GALLOP
YOUR
MAGGOT

GALLOP YOUR MAGGOT

THE ULTIMATE BOOK OF SEXUAL SLANG

Jeremy Holford

Preface by
Anne Hooper

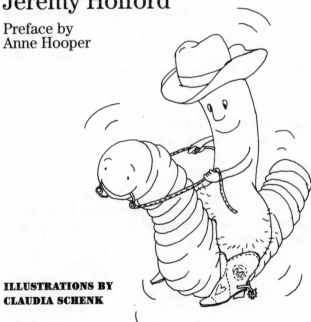

**ILLUSTRATIONS BY
CLAUDIA SCHENK**

ROBSON BOOKS

First published in Great Britain in 2005 by Robson Books, The Chrysalis Building, Bramley Road, London, W10 6SP

An imprint of **Chrysalis** Books Group plc

British Library Cataloguing in Publication Data
A catalogue record for this title is available from the British Library.

ISBN 1 86105 852 7

Printed by Clays Ltd, Bungay, Suffolk

CONTENTS

ACKNOWLEDGEMENTS

I would like to thank Anne Hooper for her help and encouragement with this book; thank-yous go to Alex Priestley and Sue Wilson for their tolerance when I talked on and on about the work. Thanks to Claudia Schenk for her witty illustrations and Barbara Phelan, Ian Allen and Mike Flynn at Robson Books for their hard work. Lastly, my thanks to L.K., N. and R., sadly no longer here to receive them.

PREFACE

Jeremy Holford, the author of this witty book of sexual slang, is my friend and co-author. A main reason for our burgeoning friendship was Jeremy's erudite and funny take on life, which complements my own sense of humour. The books we wrote together have both been documentary-comic books – mine being the documentary side, Jeremy's the comic. I wasn't surprised therefore when he told me he was compiling a book of sexual slang. It is exactly the kind of quirky research he excels at. What *did* startle me, though, as author of more than forty books on human sexuality, is the amazing wealth of language that he has come up with (no pun intended) to describe the many ways in which men and women have swung from their particular chandelier. (And no, I don't think he *did* include this particular phrase.)

Looking at the extraordinary collection of words for intercourse, oral sex, self-stimulation and the sexual organs, I now see that my books are distinctly lacking. I promise to do better next time. For example, did *you* know that a vagina has been called (during the past 300 years) a 'mole-catcher' and 'a goldfinch's nest'? No? Me neither. A 'bit on a fork' always previously conjured up pictures of a bite of tasty food – never again! And 'crinkum-crankum' I had always believed to be somebody's grumbling temperament. Apparently not. It literally means 'the winding path' and is yet *another* term for the vagina.

The value of language is that it shapes how we think. *Gallop Your Maggot* is so rich in vocabulary that I not only gained insight into how witty and tricky our ancestors must have been but also experienced a cold dollop of dismay. The terms we use for sex today are, by comparison, incredibly limited. By definition, this must mean that our contemporary view of sex is also limited. It upsets me. When you discover that, for example, the wonderful word 'callibister' is slang for 'testicles' and that a 'dead rabbit' depicts a man in his unaroused state, you begin to see why I'm getting my knickers in a twist.

It seems to me that we take sex awfully seriously these days, a viewpoint possibly responsible for the epidemic of celibacy presently sweeping the Western world. How much more light-hearted were our great-great-grandparents, as demonstrated by their sex-word treasury. And yet there *have* been leftovers of their wonderful word games in my lifetime. Most of us have, for example, heard the phrase 'faster than you can say Jack Robinson'. But how many know that 'Jack Robinson' is slang for the male member?

Any reader of D. H. Lawrence's *Lady Chatterley's Lover* remembers only too vividly the allusions made to 'John Thomas', a euphemism for the word 'penis'. But did you know that the penis gained this nickname from the fact that John Thomas was a common name for a footman? And that the flunkey class always stood when ladies were present? How tricky were the former generations, and how amusing.

My hope is that readers of this book will find the word descriptions between these covers so amusing that they can bring a lighter touch to the bedroom. If, as I suspect, we have grown too anxious about sexual performance or even feel that our entire identity rests on how well we do in bed, the comedy inherent in Jeremy's bedroom selections should cheer us up immensely. It's wonderful having a laugh when making love. *Gallop Your Maggot* helps us do so.

Anne Hooper

1. PUNSE, STRUNT AND DOODLE-SACK

Some things are better than sex, and some are worse, but there is nothing quite like it.

W. C. Fields

WORDS IN THE AIR AND ELSEWHERE

There is a reasonable chance that during the course of the day, if you are a human being moving among other humans, your existence, actions or position will offend another person. (This is especially true if you are a pedestrian, driver, cyclist or other road or pavement user.) The curse snarled or shouted at you will probably have a sexual meaning. A frequent bellow ringing down the street after you is, 'Waaan-KAA!'. You may also be accused of engaging in intercourse, anal sex and, despite visual evidence to the contrary, of being a large, mobile vagina, not to mention driving a white van.

If you are lucky, some of the same words will be whispered or moaned in a moment of shared pleasure. In either circumstance, the expressions will be part of the disappointingly small vocabulary of sexual slang in use today. The terms will be familiar and without any real impact. Their repeated use is unimaginative. You might conclude that English, the richest and most flexible language around, has an undersized sexual element.

You would be wrong.

English has plenty of terms for sexual organs and acts. The trouble is, we've forgotten them. The use of a few expressions by novelists, playwrights, and film and television writers has masked the existence of alternative, older terms that we should reclaim as our heritage.

GUSSET, LAPLAND AND PECNOSTER

This sounds like a firm of dodgy solicitors or shifty stockbrokers but is a sample of the many terms used for the female and male genitals from the sixteenth to the twentieth centuries and currently squirrelled away ready for revival. With them are other names that ought to be heard again: **punse, strunt, langolee** and **doodle-sack**.

Are you tired of the same old four-letter words for intercourse and bored by the longer, clinical phrases? Then liven up your names for playing the **national indoor game** by suggesting to your lover that you **blow the groundsels** (make love on the floor), **do a perpendicular** (standing up) or **dance the reel o' Stumpie** (for those in Scotland).

Before getting down to the **nugging** you might start off with some **firkytoodle**, including **growl-biting** and **bagpiping**.

And if you're on your own, well, just **sling your jelly**, though people may call you a **donkey flogger**.

The words and expressions dealt with in this book go back as far as the Dark Ages and forward to the 1960s, with a few later examples included. The majority of the terms are no longer in use; some are funny, unusual and appropriate and would spice up our limited slang diet. Some are basic, unimaginative and brutal; others are complex and demonstrate a pleasure in thinking up fresh descriptions. There are literary and poetic examples from professional writers hunting for ways to avoid old favourites like **cunt**, **cock** and **fuck**. There are chapters on Shakespeare's sexual language and Latin words (once upon a time, all the naughty bits in books were in Latin) to show the way slang has reached all levels of the English language and made use of other tongues and cultures.

The slang deals mainly with heterosexual activities; the older words and phrases dealing with homosexuals are pejorative, offensive and tend to repetition. The great amount of gay and lesbian slang created in recent years is outside the book's historical range and needs an author with extensive knowledge of the field.

The words and phrases included come from the United Kingdom, Ireland, Australia and New Zealand, the United States of America and Canada, and other parts of the English-speaking world. That does not mean that only English words appear; languages contributing to our sex slang range from Gaelic to Navaho, by way of Dutch, German, Italian, Old Norse, Latin and Greek.

HIDDEN, PRIVATE AND SECRET

The samples given above are vivid and amusing. There is a tendency to view slang as a swaggering, raucous and down-to-earth language, barging through the polite gatherings of other words like a randy pirate at a church picnic.

Yet Slang is not always rollicking, open and free. It is a secret language that conceals things in the way people once hid lavatories, piano legs and telephones under lace covers. There are many reasons for concealment; the elaborate criminal slang of the eighteenth century, which included fragments of Latin and Romany, and its successors during the past two hundred years, were intended to keep criminal plans secret. (Criminal slang seems to have a long life. In 1797 swindlers called themselves *sharps* and their victims *flats*, a musical-sounding choice of words. In the early part of this century, at the Cheltenham Gold Cup, I heard two prosperous but furtive men discussing a couple of flats they planned to take to the cleaners.)

Groups without criminal intentions like to create their own languages, too; these provide glue to hold the group together and a comforting sense that outsiders (adults, other groups, parents, customers) are baffled and unable to make sense of your words. A young swell of the 1850s would say, 'Bing we to Rumville,' rather than 'Let's go to London.' A modern teenager substitutes 'wicked' for 'good'. Both enjoyed the sensation of being part of a world the authorities cannot understand.

One of the most complex and lasting varieties – a provider of many contributions to the sex vocabulary – is rhyming slang, which started life in the East End of London in the 1850s. One speaker in the new style explained some terms to Henry Mayhew, the chronicler of the London poor and workers:

> Suppose I want to ask a pal to come and have a glass of rum and smoke a pipe of tobacco, and have a game at cards with some blokes at home with me, I should say, if there were any flats present, 'Splodger, will you have a *Jack-surpass* of *finger-and-thumb*, and blow your *yard of tripe* of *nosey me knacker*, and have a touch of the *broads* with me and the other *heaps of coke* at my *drum*.

Rhyming slang has expanded considerably since those days and is still growing. Although the speaker wasn't a criminal, he spoke of outsiders as flats. And he used slang to conceal his meaning.

That tendency is even more obvious when sex is the subject of discussion. The cocktail of wonder, delight, guilt, embarrassment, humour, uncertainty, longing and bewilderment making up the human emotional response to sex affects the slang. For all the macho **shag**, **screw**, **split** and **mount** terms, there are the twee descriptions of intercourse: **play mummies and daddies, nookie, make feet for children's stockings**. The stark **cunt** and **quim** are matched by **aphrodisiacal tennis court** and **boskage of Venus**. The naked **cock** becomes the uniformed **Captain Standish**, who might be a Jane Austen character.

Slang conceals with countless masks: grinning, scowling, mocking and doleful. There is a pleasure in making new words and images, and in recovering those of the past, that is part of sexual culture. Enjoy it, as you enjoy the physical acts.

WORTH ITS KEEP?

Is slang of real use? Does it deserve a place in our language? Of course it does. For every term that is cruel, sexist, ignorant and crass, there is one that has wit, charm and a strong sense of the absurd comedy of life. Slang terms, like clichés, are time machines that reduce the gap between speaking and understanding. Slang may be used in public and private as a language of intimacy and happiness as well as guile and anti-establishment feeling.

If sexual slang did not exist, what words would we use? The medical/technical terms? There is a poem, allegedly by Swinburne, that points out that anatomists have studied the body and named the parts:

> There's the vulva, the vagina and the jolly perineum,
> There's the hymen, which is sometimes found in brides,
> There's the uterus, the clitoris, the ovum and the oviducts,
> The ovaries and the lord knows what besides –

But, the poet points out, when people chat they may use a famous short word for the entire region.

Would a switch to the vocabulary of the dictionary or psychiatrist or etymologist improve the quality of life? Can you imagine issuing an invitation to cataglottism (French kissing) in a moment of passion? Or calling a one-night stand a syndyasmian incident?

How would you feel about making pillow talk the way these lovers do?

WORDPLAY

'I know some words.'

'Oh. Yes. Good. Yes. Tell me. Ooooff. Don't stop. Tell me what's in you where.'

She wriggled, not breaking stride, just letting him know who was in control of the gallop. 'Not *those* words, not the usual things it's fun to say.'

'Fine. Anything you like. Keep on, please, darling.'

A smooth transition from rapid action to a steady rise and fall of her hips. 'Well, you're mazophilous.'

'Wrong, I'm a Sagittarius.'

She stopped. 'If you're going to take the piss ...'

'No, no. What am I?'

'Mazophilous. Breasts attract you. When you slot your pintle between my bristols and shoot me a pearl necklace, that is *coitus a mammilla*. Getting a stiffie from touching my tits reveals you are subject to erotomastia.'

'You are a positive mine of information. I like more than breasts, you know.'

'I'd noticed. How about being merophilous; thighs turn you on, and pygophilous; buttocks – plus having a case of thelerethism; nipples.'

'That's a taste we share.'

'Thanks for reminding me.' Her hands moved over his body.

'Ahhh, that feels great.'

'I love male nipples; they're pretty and futile. Not like these fellows ...'

'Stroke, cup and caress but for God's sake don't squeeze hard; I want to go on having a deep voice.'

'Orchidomania,' she announced after a time.

'An abnormal interest in expensive flowers?'

'No, in balls. I'm an orchidomaniac just now, but how's about some dirty cataglottism before I head south of the border?'

(An interlewd with tongues, after which the lady was engaged in some orchidaceous osculation.)

'I've been thinking about that for hours,' she remarked. 'A case of emeronaria – that's having sexy daydreams to you.'

'Why hold back? This is the hour when we're bursting with energy.'

'Have you always been matutolagnic?'

He was bewildered and could only gawp at her.

'Liking sex in the morning,' she explained with a kindly smile.

'Oh. Yes. I find it leads to enhanced deupareunia.'

'What?!'

A moment of bliss at her confusion. 'Shared satisfaction from intercourse. Especially when it leads to synorgasmia,' was his explanation, delivered with a kindly smile.

'Both coming at the same time?'

'Correct. So let's get going. I'm so randy not even the crack of dawn is safe.'

'Darling, let's *fuck*.'

M'Lud, I rest my case for slang.

USEFUL BOOKS

Eric Partridge (1894–1979) was a scholar and slang-fanatic whose memory should be honoured by every lover of alternative languages. His most extensive work is *The Dictionary of Slang and Unconventional English*, a thorough but expensive book; there are shorter versions available, however, such as *The Penguin Dictionary of Historical Slang* and *The Concise Dictionary of Slang and Unconventional English*. Both of these are very entertaining and informative.

Jonathon Green has produced a number of books on slang, jargon and the history of dictionaries. *Slang Down the Ages: The Historical Development of Slang* is helpful as the slang is arranged by topics, for example, 'The Vagina', 'The Penis', and covers far more than sex, with chapters on drunkenness, insanity and the police. Green has also written short introductions to *The Big Book of Bodily Functions* and its companion *The Big Book of Filth*, both of which contain a great many words but minimal definitions.

Britslang: an Uncensored A–Z of the People's Language Including Rhyming Slang by Ray Puxley covers current and historical slang; the definitions are short and sharp.

The famous *Classical Dictionary of the Vulgar Tongue* by Captain Francis Grose is available in modern editions, some of which are very expensive. There are abridged paperback versions on the market.

Books with information about sexual habits and slang include Bernhardt J. Hurwood's *The Golden Age of Erotica* and *The Worm in the Bud: The World of Victorian Sexuality* by Ronald Pearsall. Walter's *My Secret Life* and reprints of *The Pearl's* erotic stories have also provided information. W. S. Baring-Gould's collection *The Lure of the Limerick* and Ed Cray's *The Erotic Muse: American Bawdy Songs* are entertaining and educational. Not all these books are currently in print but second-hand copies can be found using the Internet.

2. LADY JANE BY ANOTHER NAME

There are many more terms for the female sex organs than for the male, perhaps because men think and talk more about sex, as some psychologists and sexologists claim. Or perhaps it is because more writing by males has survived to preserve the expressions. The slang has been fixed in erotic writings, traditionally held to be both a male interest and a male product. It has been estimated that only terms for drinking and sexual intercourse outnumber those for the female genitals. The quality of the images varies from the obvious, like **gap**, **pit** and **hole** to the elaborate, such as **thatched house under the hill** and **Jack Straw's castle**, and the inventive, non-conversational literary concoctions like **aphrodisiacal tennis court** and **hypogastrian cranny**.

The emotions and sentiments conveyed are as varied as the male response to the female in all other areas of life. There are the affectionate examples – **living fountain, lady flower, puss** and **dormouse** – set against those that barely hide hatred and contempt: **dumb glutton, fires of hell** and **prick-skinner**. The last is one of a group that reveals male fear of the vagina, like **bite** and **fly-trap**.

Sources of slang are wide-ranging. The garden and the farm give us **cabbage, orchard, cauliflower** and **greens**; seafood offers the **whelk, ling** and **oyster**. The domestic scene makes its contribution with **kitchen, oven, mangle** and **saltcellar**. Streets and urban features like monuments and parks provide expressions such as **Mount Pleasant, Shooter's Hill, Marble Arch** and **Bushy Park**. The wonderful world of Mother Nature chips in with **coyote, magpie's nest, monkey** and **civet**.

There are many examples that show slang chickening out, the 'hide it away' element already mentioned. **Down there** and the various circumlocutions given under **Thing** demonstrate this practice.

Perhaps the most famous of the chicken words is **monosyllable**, believed to date from 1714 but first appearing in print in the *Classical Dictionary of the Vulgar Tongue* by Captain Francis Grose, published in London in 1785. Grose, a huge ox of a man who lived up to (and a bit over) his name, was a scholar, an expert on heraldry and paymaster of the Hampshire Militia. He gathered slang not in libraries but on the streets, in taverns and brothels, among the crowds of respectable folk and criminals at public executions and at the dinner tables of friends.

For such a jovial and curious man, Francis Grose dealt very meanly with the female anatomy. Defining the most popular term he wrote: 'C—t, a nasty word for a nasty thing'. He offered the Greek *konnos*, the Latin *cunnus* and French *con* as possible origins. (The Romans banned the use of *cunnus* as obscene, though some poets, like Horace, used the word.) Today **cunt** is generally believed to have developed from Scandinavian and Germanic languages and have links with the old Teutonic *ku* and the even more ancient Sanskrit *ga*, both meaning cow.

In the Middle Ages the word appears to have been considered vulgar but not obscene; it was 'the people's word' rather than one for the rich and educated. In both London and Oxford, streets in the red-light areas were often named Gropecunt Lane in the thirteenth century; in 1400 **cunt** was used in a surgical textbook. But by the 1490s it was considered unacceptable, though another two hundred years would pass before the use was legally forbidden. Today **cunt** is heard in films, on television and can be read in books and newspapers, but it has not regained even marginal respectability.

An anonymous poet of the 1940s offered these lines of advice on the naming of this private part:

> It's a cavern of joy you are thinking of now,
> A warm, tender field just waiting the plow.
> It's a quivering pigeon, caressing your hand,
> Or the National Anthem to make us all stand.
> Or perhaps it's a flower, a grotto, a well,
> The hope of the world or a velvety hell.
> But friend, heed this warning, beware the affront
> Of aping a Saxon: don't call it a —.

The coy '—' is the poet's work, not mine.

If your lady is bored with the better-known words, surprise her with a few helpings from this salad bowl of crisp names.

ABC. The beginning of the alphabet provides this C19 image for the place where life starts.

ACE OF SPADES. A C19 expression, often in the phrase 'Play your ace and take a Jack', which certain experts consider has something to do with sex.

ADAM'S ALTAR. Adam was the first (and only) worshipper at Eve's altar, as this C18 slang suggested.

AGREEABLE RUTS OF LIFE. This is either an invention of John Cleland in his novel *Fanny Hill* (published in 1749) or a working-class term from 1903. It depends on which history of slang you consult.

ALMANACK. This is a late-C19 word, perhaps using the idea that an almanac is frequently looked up.

ALPHA AND OMEGA. Slang from 1830 that uses a biblical reference to the beginning and end of all things.

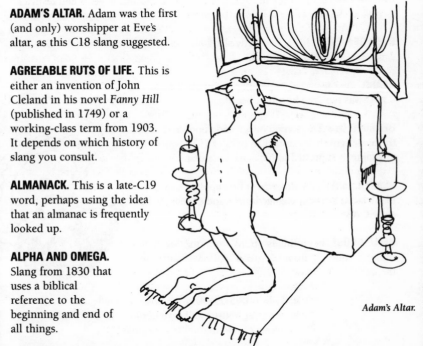

Adam's Altar.

ALTAR OF HYMEN, ALTAR OF LOVE, ALTAR OF PLEASURE. Graceful terms from the C18 and C19.

APHRODISIACAL TENNIS COURT. An elaborate term said to have been created by the Scottish writer Sir Thomas Urquhart in the C17. However as the word 'aphrodisiacal' doesn't appear in English until the C18 and Urquhart died in 1660, I am puzzled by its history.

AUNT ANNIE. A sample of C19 rhyming slang; **Aunt Annie** equals **fanny**.

AUNT MARIA. This name was briefly popular in the early C20. It must have caused some interesting confusions when Aunt Maria came a-visiting.

BAG OF TRICKS. From the mid-C19; **bag of tricks** meant the penis and testicles as well as the vulva.

BATH OF BIRTH. This is not really slang but a pleasing phrase from the C19 American poet Walt Whitman.

BEARD. First recorded in popular use in the C18; in the C19 it was replaced by **silent beard**.

Bearded Oyster

BEARDED OYSTER. A vivid image and appropriate to the oyster-guzzling Edwardian days of 1910, when this metaphor is supposed to have been popular.

BEAVER. In the C19 this was at first applied to a man's facial beard; it changed place and gender in the early C20.

BELLE-CHOSE. In an English translation, the 'lovely thing'; an offering from the great Geoffrey Chaucer in the late C14.

BEST IN CHRISTENDOM. An image created by the poet, satirist and rake Lord Rochester. Was he thinking of one woman in particular?

Beaver

BITE. A popular term that must have made nervous chaps sweat a bit between the C17 and C19. Underworld slang-sters of the C18 would say, 'The cull wapt the mort's bite', meaning that the gentleman had enjoyed the lady (who was probably a professional). The word may come from the Anglo-Saxon *byht*, meaning the fork of the legs, rather than the idea of grinding teeth.

BLACK JOKE. That is, something to be cracked. Well, they thought that was funny about 1710.

BLIND ALLEY. This is a late-C19 and early-C20 expression of no special interest.

BLUEBEARD'S CLOSET. The resting place of **Bluebeard** the penis, in C19 slang.

BONNE BOUCHE. Some educated slangster dipped into French and picked out the words generally translated as 'delicious morsel' but literally meaning 'good/pleasant mouth'.

BOSKAGE OF VENUS. Claimed as C19 slang, but it seems too poetic and arty-farty to me for street talk. I can't imagine some horny swain whispering in his lady's shell-like lughole, 'Oh Hortense, beloved, let us cop a feel of your boskage of Venus.' A boskage is also a literary term for a mass of trees and shrubs, or a thicket.

BOTANY BAY. Why use the name of the penal colony in Australia for something so desirable? Sheer perversity or fear on the part of C19 slang users?

BOTTOMLESS PIT. A phrase also used to describe hell. At one time intercourse was referred to as 'putting the devil into hell', which is a dismal view of something so enjoyable.

BREADWINNER. Like many other C19 terms, this has a practical, commercial basis.

BROWN MADAM. Based on the colour of somebody's pubic hair? Who knows? A name from the C18 and long ago forgotten. (See **Miss Brown**.)

BUCKINGER'S BOOT. A piece of slang popular from 1745–95 only, and a sad tale because Matthew Buckinger was a limbless simpleton married to a tall and lovely woman.

BUM SHOP. From mid-C19 slang, this means both a brothel and what you can hire there.

BUMBO. In use from the mid-C18 to mid-C19 and invented by slaves in the West Indies. It is also the name of a potent drink made of rum, nutmeg, sugar and water.

BUN. A dialect word for a squirrel and a short name for a bunny-rabbit as well. Sailors used to 'touch a bun for luck' before setting sail. I don't think it was squirrels they were fingering.

BUNG-HOLE. This usually meant the anus in the C18 and C19; some commentators have claimed it described quite another place.

BUSBY. The tall fur cap worn by light dragoons and hussars in the C19 and also the pubic hair.

BUSHY PARK. The pubic hair, used from 1860 onwards. The meaning of 'To take a turn/stroll/walk in Bushy Park' should be obvious to everyone. Bushy Park is also a large open space by Hampton Court Palace in London.

BUTCHER'S SHOP. A practical and commercial-sounding sample of C19 slang.

BUTTONHOLE. In use from the 1850s onwards; a buttonhole factory was a bed or a brothel.

CABBAGE, CABBAGE BED, CABBAGE FIELD, CABBAGE PATCH. One of the greens that government guidelines assure us we all need a daily helping of to stay cheerful and healthy. This late-C19 and early-C20 endearment replaced Cauliflower (see below).

CALLIBISTRY. Another example of Thomas Urquhart's word-making and derived from the word callibisters (testicles).

CANISTER. One of a number of terms used by the C18 poet Robert Burns in his collection of bawdy rhymes *The Merry Muses of Caledonia*, published after his death.

CAPE OF GOOD HOPE. A rather yearning phrase used in the latter half of the C19.

CARVEL'S RING. One of the neglected treasures of English literature is Grose's *Classical Dictionary of the Vulgar Tongue.* The book is a great source of words and tales. Like this one:

> Hans Carvel, a jealous old doctor, being in bed with his wife, dreamed that the devil gave him a ring, which, so long as he had it on his finger, would prevent his being made a cuckold: Waking, he found he had got his finger the Lord knows where.

CAT. This is a term also used for a quart mug, a whore and a lady's muff. You work out the connections.

CATHERINE WHEEL. Was this C19 image taken from the lively firework or from the grim wheel on which St Catherine was martyred? It was not in fashion for very long.

CAULIFLOWER. Before we got our greens, we were satisfied with cauliflower. Grose tells of a woman giving evidence in court who had to mention her **Venerable Monosyllable** and called it a cauliflower. The old judge snapped, 'Why call it that, madam? You could as well say "artichoke".' The lady replied, 'Not so, m'lud, for an artichoke has a bottom but a cunt and cauliflower don't.'

CELLAR, CELLARAGE, CELLAR-DOOR. Simple images of secret, dark places from the early C19.

CENTRAL FURROW. John Cleland may have invented this term for use in *Fanny Hill.*

CENTRE OF BLISS. A tender thought from the C18. It goes with rose-laden bowers, strawberries and cream and a jolly good rogering.

Cauliflower

CENTRIQUE PART. Highfalutin slang thought up in the C17 by John Donne.

CHARLIE HUNT. Rhyming slang for the vagina in the C19 and these days often innocently used in daily conversation, e.g. 'I felt a complete Charlie.'

CHUFF. Taken from North Country dialect in the C18.

CIVET. The civet is a small South Asian wildcat whose glands provide a musk-scented substance used in perfumery. The slang was invented in the C18 when civet scent was much used.

CLEFT IN THE FLESH. Somewhere between a slang term and a rather coarse euphemism, this was first recorded in the C17 and is still in use today. Cleland used it in *Fanny Hill*.

CLOVEN SPOT. Also used by Cleland in his erotic novel and, again, he may have invented the expression.

COCK ALLEY, COCK LANE. The first does not exist but the second can be found in the City of London; in the C14 it was a centre of prostitution. In 1762 the notorious 'Cock Lane Ghost' (whose name was Scratching Fanny) began haunting a house there. Dr Johnson was one of many who went to hear the strange noises the ghost made. It proved to be a hoax.

COCK-CHAFER. From the C19 and now obsolete; it suggests a painful experience was had by the man. The treadmill that C19 convicts were forced to work on not only made their legs ache but jolted and scraped them in a *most* uncomfortable fashion and was also nicknamed the **cock-chafer**.

COCK INN. A laboured pun that is said to have arrived in the C19 but is so obvious I think it must be older.

COCK PIT. Another strained piece of wordplay, based on an old English sport. Or perhaps on the cockpit of a warship; a Victorian sick joke goes:

Q: When is a newly married lady like the *Victory* at Trafalgar?
A: When her cockpit is full of bloody semen.

I suppose somebody fell off a chair laughing at that. I suppose.

COCKLES. The labia from 1700 onwards, often used in the expression **to play hot cockles**, i.e. give an intimate caress. I am surprised that the cockleshell, with its distinctly feminine shape, failed to become a slang word. Perhaps it is just hiding from me.

COGIE. A Scots word used in the C17 and C18; apparently it did not travel south of the border.

COMMODITY. A very commercial description both of the part and the woman selling it, first recorded in the C16.

CONFESSIONAL. The place for the father confessor to conduct his business.

CONJURING BOOK. A polite, rather flattering piece of slang; an attempt to pun on 'conjuring' and 'conjugal' has been suggested by some writers.

CONO. A slang term derived from Spanish and popular in the South-west of the USA during the 1940's.

Coney

CONY, CONEY. The medieval word for a rabbit and, from the C16 to the C18, for a fool, among other things. People envy and despise rabbits for their lively and highly productive sex lives; dire warnings have been put in verse, for example:

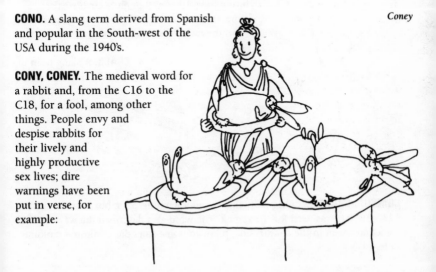

Children, have you heard about the rabbits?
They have such strange and vile habits.
Oh kids, I daren't disclose to you
The dreadful things *some* rabbits do.

During the Roman Empire young women were encouraged to eat plenty of rabbit to make them more fertile and randy.

COOZE. Used in the USA for the **doodle-sack** from the 1920s.

CORNER CUPBOARD. Essential furnishing for the C19 home; the **corner** was the groin where the cupboard was placed.

COUNTY DOWN. A piece of verbal compression from the C19; the slang means both the vagina and pubic hair.

COYNTE. A literary spelling of **cunt** from the C19; Sir Richard Burton employed it in his translations of erotic classics.

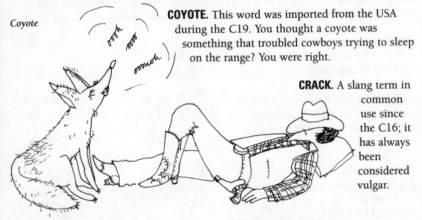

Coyote

COYOTE. This word was imported from the USA during the C19. You thought a coyote was something that troubled cowboys trying to sleep on the range? You were right.

CRACK. A slang term in common use since the C16; it has always been considered vulgar.

CRINKUM-CRANKUM. Originally this meant a winding path, but from 1770–1870 it was used for the vagina. The word also described the wavy wall sometimes seen in the countryside; there are some splendid crinkum-crankums in Essex.

Crown

CROWN OF SENSE/THE SENSES. Another of those phrases that sounds more poetic than slangy; this one dates from the 1680s and may be the work of Lord Rochester.

CUCKOO'S NEST. An Irish term, appearing in a famous C19 folksong.

CUNNY. This looks like a variation on the next term in the list, but is actually linked to **cony**; it has been in use from the C17 to the present day.

CUNT. Come on, you didn't think this would be left out, did you? The most frequently used term of description and abuse and even, at times, of affection.
As pointed out, **cunt** was a simple descriptive and respectable word until the C15, when its status began to decline as Puritanism arrived and folk became more genteel. The fine old word has a variety of spellings, including 'coynte', 'cunde', and 'quente'. Whichever you pick, do make sure to start it with a 'c' and don't copy this silly sailor:

> There was a young maid of Bombay
> Who was put in the family way
> By the mate of a lugger,
> An ignorant bugger,
> Who always spelt cunt with a K.

Cuckoo's Nest

Variants include cuntlet, cunt-hole, cunnikins and the backslang tenuc.

CUPID'S ALLEY. Like his mother Venus, Cupid features in a variety of expressions; this description of **Aunt Annie** comes from the 1750s. Other examples are Cupid's anvil, Cupid's cave, Cupid's cloister and Cupid's cupboard.

CUSH. Apparently based on the Arabic for vulva, this was a component of 1950s slang. As a point of interest, 'Cushy' is a derivation of the Hindi word for pleasant.

CUT AND COME AGAIN. An unending supply conjured by some hopeful C19 slangmongers.

DELL. From the 1550s, this stood for a wanton girl and what she owned that men were wanton.

DICKY-DI-DO, DIDDY-DI-DO. I thought this expression only appeared in the old rugger-bugger song 'The Hairs on Her Dicky-di-do' (tune, 'The Ash Grove') but have been informed that it was in jocular use between 1900–40.

DOODLE-SACK. Originally an English term for a bagpipe; the word was used with a sexual meaning in the C18.

DORMOUSE. A dormouse is a small, furry mammal that spends a large part of its life asleep. Hmmm. I kept one (the animal) as a pet when I was a boy; it was bad-tempered and had a nasty bite. Hmmm once again.

DOWN THERE, DOWNSTAIRS. Coy talk from the days of Queen Victoria. The first is still used today.

DOWNSHIRE. This is another example of the genteel slang in use during the Victorian period.

DOWNY BIT. Dates from 1880 and was more often used to describe an attractive woman rather than just one of her features.

DUMB GLUTTON. Silent and always ready for feeding – the ideal woman for some men. This was a popular term from the mid-C18 to mid-C19.

DUTCH CLOCK. At first this meant a warming-pan; later in the C19 it was used for the part of a woman that might well make a man hot under the sheets.

EVE'S CUSTOM-HOUSE. The implication of this C18 slang was that every man who entered paid duty, one way or another.

EYE THAT WEEPS MOST WHEN IT IS BEST PLEASED. G. A. Stevens cooked up this phrase in the late C18; I cannot imagine any lover whispering it (or shouting it) in or out of a passionate moment.

FACTOTUM. The pudenda of a promiscuous woman, in a fanciful pun; *totum* is Latin meaning 'all', and 'Fac' is easily changed to another word.

FANCY BIT, FANCY PIECE. Both from the C19; the second was more often applied to the entire lady.

FANNY. A name first used around 1860, which may have been lifted from the novel *Fanny Hill* or a tin mug used for rum by the Royal Navy. Rare variations are artful fanny and fanny fair. In the USA, of course, Fanny has a very different meaning; do not confuse them. Over there the term means bottom.

FARE-DANIEL, FART-DANIEL. These are C19 dialect terms; originally a fare-daniel was the weakest piglet in a litter, often taken into the farmhouse kitchen to be reared. **Fart-daniel** is probably a misprint but it is colourful. Unflattering, but colourful.

FIDDLE. A musical image first employed in 1800. See **bow** in the next chapter.

FIE FOR SHAME. Used by C19 schoolgirls, according to Jonathon Green. Fie and oh-fie were in use at a convent school in Essex as late as the 1960s.

FIG. From the shape and, more importantly, the look of a split fig, which resembles the labia and vagina. The slang was first recorded in English during the mid-C19 but goes back to Roman times.

FIRELOCK, FIREPLACE, FIREWORK. All from the C19, all indicating or implying infection with gonorrhoea, a.k.a. the clap, flame and the Covent Garden ague.

FIRES OF HELL. The sort of kill-joy, scared phrase snarled by frustrated Puritans. This dates from about 1855.

FISH, BIT OF FISH, FISH MARKET. These are all C19 expressions with inspirations drawn from the moistness and scent of fish. A particular species may be mentioned, as in 'a bit of skate' or **ling**.

FLESHY PART. In 1899 this was the opening of a polite expression for a buttock, 'the fleshy part of the thigh', and was used by newspapers to indicate where a British general fighting in the Boer War had been shot. Slang shifted the term to the region where it was needed.

FLOWER OF CHIVALRY. Highfalutin words from the C19, with a hidden pun for the sharp-witted, chivalry being the art of riding.

FLOWERPOT. A bit of horticultural imagery from the 1880s.

FLY BY NIGHT. This C19 phrase was generally used to indicate contempt for women; the idea of witches flying their broomsticks and debtors sneaking off without paying their bills (a non-sexual use of the term) lay behind the slang.

FLY-TRAP. This was in use during the C19. Later on the meaning changed to 'mouth'. But the change had not taken place when this appeared in *The Pearl* in 1880: 'La! Polly has got no hair on her fly-trap yet.'

FOBUS. This word for the vagina was originally the C16 equivalent of 'fogy', as in 'old/young fogey'; the sexual meaning was not added until the 1890s.

FORK, BIT ON A. The vagina as a tasty snack in the 1860s.

FRONT ATTIC, FRONT DOOR, FRONT GARDEN, FRONT WINDOW. All these came into use during the C19 at a time when more and more people were buying their own homes.

FRONT-DOOR MAT. The pubic hair, 1880–1900.

FRONT-GUT. A coarse lump of slang used from 1890–1910.

Front-door Mat

FRUTEX VULVARIA. Elaborate Latin term used from the 1730s by people wishing to show off.

FUMBLER'S HALL. An address known to the inept, the impotent and the drunk of the C18, who struggled to enter but failed.

FUNNIMENT. Punning on 'fundament' perhaps? A C19 usage that has disappeared.

FUNNY BIT. In use in the middle of the C19 and probably the inspiration for the previous entry.

GALLIMAUFRY. The female genitals, a mistress and a stew made of all the odds and ends to be found in the larder. The sexual meanings date from the C16; the culinary one is found in Grose in 1785.

GAP. The word was employed by the medical profession as an anatomical description but became slang in the late C18.

GAPE/GAPER OVER THE GARTER. One of those coarse C19 nicknames, which are best forgotten.

GARDEN, GARDEN OF EDEN. This is a two-faced expression going back to the C16. It can be slang but has been used in poetry, which of course makes it respectable. The same dual status applies to **rose**. (The labia are the 'garden gate'.)

GARDEN-HEDGE. This, on the other hand, was always considered vulgar and means the pubic hair in late-C19 and early-C20 slang.

GASH. First used as a name in the C18 and still going strong. In the Royal Navy the word means anything going spare, unclaimed or left lying about right and theft.

GATE OF LIFE. Robert Burns gave the world this metaphor in the late 1790s.

GINCH. This began as a British dialect word 'ginchy', meaning something very good. It changed to a term for the vagina in 1950s America.

GOLDFINCH'S NEST. Given the rather unpleasant nature of much C19 slang, this example from 1827 is quite charming.

GREENS. A term that these days usually stands for fucking, as in 'He's getting his greens from Mrs Brown,' but occasionally it does refer to the vagina. First used about 1845.

GROMMET. An American item shipped into UK slang in the 1850s; its use has never been widespread.

GROVE OF EGLANTINE. A flowery effort by the poet Thomas Carew (and, by the way, you pronounce his name 'Carey'). Eglantine is the wild rose or, according to some botanists, honeysuckle.

GROVE OF SWEET RETIREMENT. An early-Victorian phrase and literary-sounding. Sometimes the first word was spelt 'gro(o)ve' to make sure even the lackwits understood what was being referred to.

GROWL. About 1890 some lazy person shortened the rhyming slang 'growl and grunt' and the new name caught on. Nobody tried 'grunt' on its own.

GRUMMET, GRUMMIT. A maritime word that came ashore in 1865. Ahoy there, example of the use:

> Scene: Two ladies chatting in a pornographic memoir of the day
> 'What are you sitting there for?'
> No reply.
> 'What's that basin there for?'
> No reply.
> 'You have been washing your grummit?'
> No reply.
> 'What have you been washing it for?'
> 'I was hot.'

GUSSET. An obvious anatomical analogy borrowed from the tailor's trade and worn from the C17 to mid-C19.

GUT-ENTRANCE. Not the most endearing or charming of terms; it turned up about 1830 but did not stay long.

GYVEL. Another one from Burns; how did the man find time to write *Ode to a Haggis*?

HAIRY ORACLE. The oracle may be a play on the idea of an O; **hairy oracle** dates from the last part of the C19 and is no longer in use. But you could change that.

HAIRY RING. A metaphor to be found in the *Festival of Love* published in 1770:

> Your husband gave to you a ring,
> Set round with jewels rare;
> You gave him a better thing –
> A ring set round with hair.

Gusset

That was addressed to Lady T—re—l by a Mr S—e. I wonder what she thought of the verse.

HAIRY WHEEL. In Australia from 1860 this referred to the female anatomy; in the UK it meant the male. One nation is very confused, but which?

HAIRYFORDSHIRE. This is a laboured 1850s pun based on the county Herefordshire.

HALF MOON. A simple but pleasing comparison dating from the C17. It was also the name of a type of wig.

HALFPENNY, HA'PENNY. The vagina in the days when decimal coinage was something reserved for those very peculiar people inhabiting the Continent.

HARBOUR OF HOPE. Yearning, even wistful, language from about 1840. The phrase was at times truncated to **harbour**.

HEY-NONNY-NO. From the 1590s to the 1750s this was also used as a popular chorus in folksongs and madrigals. Perhaps more of a literary phrase than slang.

HOLE. Slang at its most basic descriptive level in the C19. This is often found in the phrase 'He likes his bit of hole.'

HOLE(S) OF CONTENT. Employed from the mid-C16 until the C19 and all-encompassing, with nothing left for the imagination to do.

HOLY OF HOLIES. A term calculated to offend the religious; in popular use 1890–1910.

HOME SWEET HOME. This is not exactly slang but a quote from an 1823 song by John Howard Payne:

> Mid pleasures and palaces though we may roam,
> Be it ever so humble, there's no place like home …
> Home, home, sweet, sweet home!
> There's no place like home!

The expression was first recorded in a sexual sense in about 1870.

HONEYPOT. A rather charming late C17/early C18 word for the vagina. The honey in question was semen. In his song 'Brush up your Shakespeare' Cole Porter said 'Just recite an occasional sonnet/And your lap will have honey upon it', and who am I to disagree?

Horse Colla

HORSE COLLAR. An unflattering name from the C19 those unfamiliar with harness need to picture a large leather loop, stuffed to keep it stiff, and big enough to pass over a horse's head and neck. Now you understand why it's unflattering.

> A lady with features cherubic
> Was famed for her area pubic.
> When they asked her its size,
> She asked with surprise,
> 'Are you speaking of square feet or cubic?'

HYPOGASTRIAN CRANNY. Sir Thomas Urquhart at it again, cooking up a word from the Greek *hypogastrium* meaning the part of the body below the belly and above the genitals. I think his sense of direction was out of order when he invented this.

INGLENOOK. Some mid-C19 home-loving chap thinking of a warm and cosy nook by the fireplace thought this one up, I'd wager.

INLET. A sailing or literary term rather than slang; it enjoyed a short vogue in the middle of the C19. 'I came to the conclusion that she was born loose at her inlet ...' wrote Walter (see **lubricious avenue**) of one mistress's anatomy.

IT. Stark, simple and the complete removal of all personality and context. A C19 use, generally as 'to do it'. The word shifted its meaning and became a synonym for 'sex appeal'; Rudyard Kipling used it in a 1904 short story *Mrs Bathurst* to describe the heroine's unconscious attraction for men. In the 1920s Elinor Glyn's novel *It* made the term very popular. When the book was filmed in 1928, the star Clara Bow at once became the 'It Girl'.

Which is a lead-in (in a sneaky way) to a limerick I can't find another place for:

> The new cinematic emporium
> Is not just a super-sensorium
> But a highly effectual
> Heterosexual
> Mutual masturbatorium.

ITCHER OR ITCHING JENNY. Both terms date from the first decade of the C20. They may indicate that the organ in question is diseased.

JACK STRAW'S CASTLE. Straw was the leader of the revolting peasants who invaded London in 1381, but this name only became popular around 1700 and was forgotten after 1900, so how did it arise? There is a famous pub by Hampstead Heath called Jack Straw's Castle, so there may be a link there. Pregnant women were said to have 'Jack in the low cellar'. Silly and unimportant men were, of course, known as 'Jack Straws'.

JELLY BAG. This meant both the female pudenda and the scrotum to slangsters from the late C17, but which came first, the hen or the eggs?

JIGGER. Slang from the C19 that could also mean a penis or a lock. These days it is often used as a measure of alcohol.

JOCK. When first recorded in 1790, the word applied to both female and male sex organs; after 1880 it became exclusively masculine.

JOCKUM. This was first a name for the female pubic hair, created in the C16. Then it stood for the penis until the late C19.

JUSTUM. It seems this was another first for Thomas Urquhart, a man with much time on his hands and no idea of a better use for his fist. A literary oddity rather than a popular description.

KETTLE. The author Thomas D'Urfey was apparently the first to use this word in a sexual fashion, in the 1680s.

KITCHEN. A word that became fashionable in the 1860s when Mrs Beeton's famous cookery book was published. I am not suggesting that Isabella Beeton (who died too young at the age of 29) created the usage, but she might have focused interest on the kitchen. In the American blues a 'kitchen mechanic' is a good lover.

LADDER. An unimaginative piece of C19 slang now applied to tears in tights and stockings, which makes good sexual sense. The only limerick I know featuring a ladder is:

Ladder

> While Titian was mixing rose madder,
> His model reclined on a ladder,
> Her position to Titian
> Suggested coition;
> So he leapt up the ladder and had 'er.

LADY FLOWER. Charming and very poetic, which is hardly surprising, since Walt Whitman made it up.

LADY JANE. A popular slang term for the female genitals first noted around 1850. In polite society at the end of that century the expression meant a jolly, handsome woman. The name enjoyed a revival in the 1960s when *Lady Chatterley's Lover*, which makes great use of it, was published.

> When Lady Jane became a tart
> It almost broke her father's heart;
> But blood is blood and race is race,
> And so to mitigate disgrace,
> He bought a most expensive beat,
> From Asprey's down to Old Bond Street.

A little poem to show that, even in the sordid commercial world, good breeding does count.

LAPLAND. From circa 1840 onwards this meant not only the organ but also the company of women.

LEADING ARTICLE. Not a term thought up by an editor or reporter but a C19 grocer's description of an artfully displayed item that would lead customers on to buy other things.

LEAK. In the C18 this meant a woman; from the C19 onwards, urination. Here is a mid-C20 verse offering from the USA:

> A plumber from Lowater Creek
> Was called in by a dame with a leak;

> She looked so becoming,
> He fixed *all* her plumbing
> And didn't emerge for a week.

LEATHER. This was first recorded in the C16 and continued to be used until the early C20.

LEATHER LANE. A nickname heard from late in the C18 until about 1914. It appears in the popular music-hall song 'If it Wasn't for the 'ouses in Between' performed by Gus Elan. In the song a costermonger tries to make his slum yard look like the countryside:

Leather Lar

> We're as countrified as can be wiv a clothes prop for a tree,
> The tub-stool makes a rustic little stile;
> Ev'ry time the bloomin' clock strikes there's a cuckoo sings to me,
> And I've painted up 'To Leather Lane a mile'.
>
> CHORUS:
>
> Oh, it really is a wery pretty garden,
> And Chingford to the eastward could be seen;
> Wiv a ladder and some glasses,
> You could see to 'ackney Marshes,
> If it wasn't for the 'ouses in between.

The countryside is seldom far from the Englishman's mind.

LEAVING SHOP. An unlicensed pawnbroker's, according to the newspapers of 1857, based on the obvious idea that you only visit a pawnshop to leave something behind.

LING. A sea-life metaphor; the ling is a cousin of the cod and large ones can weigh 100lb. This is C16 slang in Great Britain and C20 in Australia, which must be cultural diffusion at its slowest. **Ling-grappling** meant intercourse and masturbation (see Chapters 5 and 6).

LITTLE SISTER. Almost polite talk rather than slang, she joins the family about 1840 and is blessed with a **little brother** in the next chapter.

Ling

LIVING FOUNTAIN. A charming term created by the poet Robert Herrick (you know: 'Gather ye rosebuds while ye may', etc., etc.) in his 1648 poem *To Dianeme*:

> Show me thy feet; show me thy legs, thy thighs;
> Show me those Fleshy Principalities;
> Show me that Hill (where smiling Love doth sit)
> Having a living fountain under it.

LOBSTER-POT. The shape of this trap must have caused a slangster to make the comparison. It conjures up the troubling notion that once you're in you'll never get out again.)

> There was a young harlot of Kew
> Whose vagina was filled up with glue,
> Said she, with a grin,
> 'If they pay to get in,
> They can pay to get out again, too.'

LOCK, LOCK OF LOCKS. Basic imagery used in the C18, with the obvious male counterpart being the **key**.

LONG EYE. An optic that first gazed on the scene in the 1850s. It sounds like an American Indian chief to me; Long Eye, great leader of the Potawatomi, fearless warrior and father of

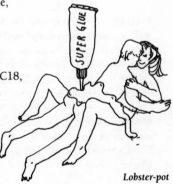

Lobster-pot

his people. Come to think of it, that should be Mighty Squaw Long Eye, Mother of Thousands, All-seeing and All-knowing.

LOVE LANE. Rather coy, less slang than circumlocution. Generally used in a phrase 'take a stroll in Love Lane', a popular spot for a ramble during the late C19 and early C20. It still is, by all accounts.

LOW COUNTRIES, LOWLANDS. A little simple imagery from about 1750.

LUBRICIOUS AVENUE. A thoroughfare frequented by literary coves from 1860–1900.

Walter (real name unknown) wrote in *My Secret Life* (his sexual autobiography): '… we spent in rapture, almost before we had begun the glorious to and fro of my prick in her lubricious avenue'.

LUCKY BAG. This was the C19 precursor of today's lucky dip, but did not feature at children's parties.

MADGE, MADGE HOWLETT. A brace of long-forgotten country expressions. Howlet means a baby owl, soft and warm and sweet.

Magpie's Ne

MAGPIE'S NEST. The magpie builds a large, domed nest, according to birders. From the C18 until the early C20 enough resemblance was observed to keep this name in use. Or maybe it was just idleness.

MALKIN. In Scotland this was the name for a cat as well as a pussy, first noted in the latter sense about 1540. Shakespeare knew the word; in *Macbeth* the First Witch says, 'I come, Grey Malkin', but we won't go into that here. 'Rough Malkin' was also used in Scotland in the C16.

MANGLE. A mangle's wooden rollers squeezed wet clothes dry. Was something like that in the mind of the slangmaker who introduced this usage in 1860? Fond memories of the delicious **devil's bite** (see Chapter 5) may have inspired him or her.

MANHOLE. An example of basic, not very inventive slang from about 1870.

MARBLE ARCH. Apart from the obvious physical attribute of the arch, this could be a punning reference to the Arch being the entrance to Hyde Park. Eric Partridge, compiler of the great *Dictionary of Slang and Unconventional English*, proposed this theory about the mid-C19 term.

MARY. A word appearing in several dialects and claimed by some as a Romany term, though I can find no evidence for that.

MARY JANE. Slang based, it seems, on an affectionate nickname from 1840 or so; later on the name was applied to marijuana.

MASTERPIECE. There is a mixed message in this slang dating from the C18. A masterpiece is a treasured item, the acme of excellence, but sexually it is the part of a woman that belongs to her master, whether husband or employer. Oh well, the lady could always tease the man and be a master-baiter.

MEDLAR. A word in vogue for about two hundred years from 1660. In Standard English a medlar is a pear-shaped fruit that can be eaten only when it is overripe and close to rotten.

MELTING-POT. An image in use during the C19; at the same time 'melted butter' was a popular term for semen.

MICHAEL. Australian rhyming slang (think Michael Hunt – OK?). As ever, this has the shorter versions Mick and Mickey. All date from the 1930s.

MIDLANDS, THE. This name was popular with witty folk in the 1830s.

MILK JUG. A slang application from the C18 when 'milking' meant ejaculation. Related expressions are milker, milk pail and milk pan.

MILL. Yet again a word from Mr Burns's mind, linked with the observation that a lot of grinding goes on in a mill. The poet Swinburne (it is claimed) penned this little rhyme about a young woman who took her mill to a mill:

There was a young girl of Aberystwyth
Who took grain to the mill to get grist with,
The miller's son, Jack,
Laid her flat on her back
And united the organs they pissed with.

MILLINER'S SHOP. A milliner's shop sells hats, ribbons and fancy trimmings, so can be considered a feminine sort of place. The phrase (both slang and Standard English) seems to be little used these days.

MILT SHOP. Milt is fish roe and the idea or appearance of the roe gave some creative person the idea for a new description.

MINGE. Is this adapted from a Romany word, *minj*, or from a country dialect? No one seems sure, but it has been around since early in the C19 and is now held respectable enough not to be bleeped out on reality TV shows.

MIRACULOUS CAIRN. The *mons veneris* in the mid-C19, when a golden age of mountaineering was just beginning.

MIRACULOUS PITCHER. According to Grose's dictionary, the miracle is that 'the object holds water with its mouth downwards'. A deflowered woman was said to have 'cracked her pitcher'. Both expressions were in use about 1750–1800.

MISS BROWN. Grose recorded this in his dictionary, too; by about 1820 the name had been forgotten.

MISS HORNER. This C19 term contains the ideas of being horny, Jack Horner putting his thumb into the pudding, and the Devil, Old Horney.

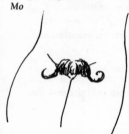

Mo

MISS LAYCOCK. A pun on **cock** (see Chapter 3), appearing in the language at the end of the C18. Like **mossy face** it was underworld slang and was revived by Timberlake Wertenbaker in her 1988 play *Our Country's Good*.

MO. An Antipodean abbreviation for the pubic zone and its cover; **mo** is short for moustache.

MOLE-CATCHER, MOLE TRAP. The image is rural and obvious; moles live in dark tunnels and to catch one you must enter the tunnel. Of course, real mole-catchers don't crawl down tunnels but set traps on the surface. Slang is illogical and prefers a good picture to reality. Let us be thankful for that.

MONEY. A precious commodity that everyone wants and recognised as such by this 1780s term. It was often applied to very young girls and could also be a warning: 'Beware, miss, or you'll show your money.'

MONEY-BOX, MONEY-MAKER, MONEY-SPINNER. Distinctly commercial thoughts are behind these examples of C19 and C20 slang.

MONKEY. In the C19 this was almost always used in the phrase 'where the monkey sleeps'. This is said to be in use today, but I have never heard or read it, except in those books about slang that claim it is in use today.

MONOSYLLABLE. This is a genteel name for **cunt** and may have been used as early as 1714, though it was put in a dictionary only in 1785. **Monosyllable** has not been used extensively since about 1880.

MONS MEG. There is an ancient and venerated cannon in Edinburgh Castle called Mons Meg. The gun dates back to the C15 but the slang only to the C19.

MOSSY FACE. An example of C18 thieves' slang brought back to life in the 1980s by Timberlake Wertenbaker in her play *Our Country's Good*. It is a slang term for the card the **Ace of Spades**, too.

MOSSY GROTTO. Pornographers' literary expression from the 1880s.

MOSSY RETREAT. Another literary term used by porn-slingers, as witness *The Pearl* in 1880: 'I felt Miss Arundel's compressed thighs relax in their resistance, and she gave a spasmodic sigh as I victoriously advanced my rude hand to her mossy retreat.'

MOTHER NATURE'S TUFTED TREASURE. An elaborate phrase devised in the C19 but too long-winded for our high-speed modern age.

MOTHER OF ALL SAINTS. Not to mention all sinners, of course. Grose's dictionary recorded this in 1785. A variation on it is 'mother of all souls'. For men of a secretive nature with a yen for fancy dress and curious handshakes there is also 'mother of masons'.

MOTHER OF ST PATRICK. An Anglo-Irish version of the previous entry that made me laugh, so I gave it a space of its own. When the alcoholic Irish writer Brendan Behan was dying, he looked at the nun nursing him and said, 'Thanks for all you've done, sister. May you be the mother of a bishop.'

MOTTE. A literary/cultured name for the Mount of Venus, employing a word that describes a mound with a Norman castle on top. Walter is fond of **motte**: 'There is no more thrilling sight than a woman sitting or lying down naked, her cunt hidden by her thighs and only indicated by the shade from the curls of her motte.'

MOUNT-FAUCON. Slang expert Jonathon Green attributes this to the C16 author John Florio and describes the term as 'positively bodice-ripping'. Hear, hear.

MOUNT PLEASANT. The London district was not actually named in honour of the Mount of Venus, but the 1880s slangmakers did not let that inhibit them. As a description of a region and an invitation, this is charming. (PS: I know that a number of Mount Pleasants exist up and down the British Isles; the London one was the earliest I found mention of. No disrespect is intended to, for example, Liverpool's Mount Pleasant.)

MOUSE-TRAP. This term, which conjures painful images, came into use in about 1850 but seems forgotten.

MOUSER. A **mouser** is, of course, a cat. Which is a pussy. Ah, you've caught on.

MOUTH THANKLESS, THE. Sir Walter Scott is alleged to have thought this up, presumably in the intervals between churning out his turgid novels.

MOUTH THAT CANNOT BITE. For any male haunted by the Freudian nightmare of the fanged fanny, the dread *vagina dentata,* which with one chomp can render him useless, this phrase must offer great comfort. At least, it did from 1750 to 1850.

MOUTH THAT SAYS NO WORDS. Another of G. A. Stevens's efforts and probably never in general use, except by G. A. Stevens.

MUFF. Soft, furry and good for keeping the hands warm, yes, a muff was an object the slangsters could not ignore. Their fresh definition was applied in the late C17 and clung to life until about 1910. A toast for a good wedding night went 'Here's to the happy wearing of your muff.'

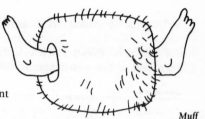

Muff

MUMBLE-PEG. A C19 expression of uncertain origin; it has been suggested that the name refers to an old variety of mole trap. I suppose that sounds as likely as anything.

MUTTON. In the 1670s this meant the vagina; well before that, as early as 1518, the word meant a whore, as commonly used in the phrase 'laced mutton'.

NAF. An example of backslang for fan, i.e. **fanny**, from circa 1845.

NAGGIE, NAGGY. Until the 1780s this meant a pony or small horse and was confined to country dialects. Then somebody decided there were not enough names around and borrowed it for a new role. It was also used for male organs.

NAMELESS. The ultimate in avoidance and part of C19 slang.

NANTY CRACKLING. The first word is Palary (theatre and circus) slang for 'nothing' or 'none' and the absence of crackling (hard, burnt skin) in this particular circumstance is to be commended.

NEEDLECASE. A home for the **needle**, which was a name for the penis from the C17 onwards. But **needlecase** did not arrive until the C19, along with **needle-woman**, meaning prostitute.

NEST, NEST IN THE BUSH. Both terms were put into print by literary men in the C18 – Burns (again) and G. A. Stevens (also again) being responsible.

NETHER EYE. This is Chaucer getting low down and dirty; he also gave us 'nether end' but not 'nether dimple' or 'nether smile'.

NOCK. John Florio used this in his books circa 1590.

NONESUCH, NONSUCH. The female sex organs and a palace that Elizabeth I often slept in. The sexual meaning dates from circa 1720.

NONNY-NO. The vulva in C16 slang.

NOTCH. A basic comparison from the late C18; in the following century it became more elaborate as 'nick in the notch'. Walter, the unidentified C19 sex addict, used the term often, for example: 'I slipped my hand up her clothes, felt big thighs and a fully haired notch … then I put my pego into her hand. "Let's fuck, my darling – let me do it."'

NUMBER-NIP. I know nothing about this word except that it dates from the C19 and sounds bloody painful.

OLD DING. Does this have anything to do with 'ding', meaning to hit or strike? Nobody knows for sure, but that did not prevent the expression from being in use in the late C19 and early C20.

OLD HAT. This dates from the C17; it was Grose in 1785 who explained the image – 'because it is frequently felt'.

OLD LADY. Affectionate if somewhat patronising, the endearment was in use in the C19 and the early years of the C20 and was revived (usually in the sense of a girlfriend) by the beatniks and Hell's Angels in the 1950s and the hippies in the 1960s.

OMNIBUS. Because it takes on all passengers, in the view of a slangster of 1840.

OPEN C. Plain speaking and simple imagery from the first half of the C19.

ORANGE. A description from the time of Charles II's restoration to the throne and perhaps in compliment to his mistress Nell Gwynn's trade. Cue for old joke: 'I say, you with the oranges, what are you selling? Yourself or the oranges?'

ORCHARD. An example of the rural element in slang, demonstrating the British fondness for the countryside. This appeared in the C19 when more and more farm workers were heading for the cities.

OVEN. First popular in the C18, this has survived in the slang for pregnant – having a bun in the oven. A country proverb said, 'He who has hidden in the oven knows where to find a son or daughter.'

OYSTER. An obvious comparison put on record in the C19 but almost certainly much older. There is supposed to have been an erotic magazine called *The Oyster* but I have been unable to trace it so far. *The Pearl* did exist from 1879–82 and published such gems as 'Lady Pockingham, or They All Do It', 'Swivia, or The Briefless Barrister' and 'Sub-Umbra, or Sport Among the She-Noodles'.

There was a ballad called 'As Oyster Nan Stood by Her Tub' telling of Nan's labours shucking shellfish in the inn's kitchen. The wine-waiter arrives and lends a helping hand, among other things. When a customer calls for him and the waiter shouts a response, Nan adds her own remark:

> I'm coming, coming, Sir, says he;
> My dear, and so am I, says she, Sir.

From that day on the pair work as a team and Nan regularly '… shuts and opens like an oyster'.

Oysters (shellfish) are considered to be potent aphrodisiacs; Casanova swallowed them by the dozen. In the 1980s the high zinc level in oysters was discovered to be good for the sex drive and the origin of their aphrodisiac fame. As an experiment a group of male patients in a Michigan hospital received extra zinc and their libidos improved.

PANCAKE. A delicacy served up in the C17, probably with much tossing involved.

PARSLEY BED. Generally appearing in the phrase for the sexual act to 'take a stroll in the parsley bed' and part of the language from 1600. Little girls were supposed to come from the parsley bed, and little boys from the nettle bed or from under the gooseberry bush.

In 'Lady Pockingham, or They All Do It' the old Marquis of Pockingham is much disappointed that his wife's adultery with the servant James only produced a daughter and not the hoped-for son; the old aristo '... wished her to let James cultivate her parsley bed for another crop, which might be more in accordance with the marquis's wishes'.

PART OF INDIA. In the C17 the poet John Donne saw the shape of India on a chart and at once made this connection. Was it Ogden Nash who made this comment?

Penwiper

> Donne is fun,
> But Chaucer's coarser.

PENWIPER. In the days before fountain pens and ballpoints, pens were dipped in ink-wells and would become quite messy, so a soft cloth was used to clean them. The fact that **pen** was mid-C19 slang for the penis has nothing to with the matter, I am sure.

PERIWINKLE. This could mean the evergreen plant with pale blue flowers or the edible shellfish. My money is on the mollusc. The slang is from the 1890s.

PIGEONHOLE. One of the less frequently used terms from the C19; it has an official and bureaucratic air.

PINTLE-CASE. The word **pintle** was an acceptable term for the penis from circa 1100 to 1750. Of course, the **pintle** had to be stored somewhere, so why not in a case? The slangmongers were slow off the mark with this one, which did not emerge until the C19, by which time **pintle** was out of fashion.

PIT, BOTTOMLESS PIT, PIT HOLE, PIT OF DARKNESS. The first term goes back to the C17; the others are from the C18 and the first part of the C19. **Pit** and **pit hole** suggest mining; how those poor miners suffered, enduring long hours labouring in the pits. **Pit of darkness** has been used for 'hell' and is one of those morbid, puritanical bits of slang that are depressing.

PLEASURE BOAT. When Queen Victoria married Prince Albert in 1838 there was considerable public disapproval. One of the queen's cousins wrote a smutty verse about Albert and many jokes were made about the couple. A popular song describes Albert dreaming of a jaunt on a pleasure boat and waking up '… to find himself aboard *The British Queen*'.

POND. The word acquired a sexual dimension in the C17. It was one of the slang words Shakespeare used in his plays, in this case *The Winter's Tale*.

POOR MAN'S BLESSING. A C19 expression suggesting that be he never so humble a chap can always find something to be thankful for. One wonders what the blessing herself thought of the matter.

PRANNY. From the late C19, a term always used contemptuously and looking like a blend of **prat** and **fanny**. It is sometimes spelled 'prannie'.

PRAT, PRATT. Nowadays the word usually refers to the buttocks, but it was used for the vagina in the late C19. When it first appeared in the C16 it meant a tinder-box.

PRICK-SKINNER. Male verbal aggression covering male physical fear in the 1880s and 1890s. Other descriptions of the vagina involving the popular **prick** are prick-holder, prick-purse and prick-scourer, all from 1600–1790. Prick-tube was in use during the second part of the C19: 'Her massive thighs shut me off from the prick-tube as closely as it if had been a closed door.'

PRIVY PARADISE. From the C19 and with an air of ownership about it. The slang is related to the expression 'private property', used for both female and male sex organs.

PUDDLE. Given a capital, letter the word is a nickname for the Atlantic Ocean; with a lowercase letter it acquires another meaning.

PUMP. A sample of C18 slang that went out of use about 1850. Pumpdale, an older form, was recorded in 1699.

PUNDU. A South African vagina dating from the 1950s.

PUNSE. This is Yiddish slang from London in the late C19; it was sometimes rendered as poonse or punce. The male counterpart is **putz**.

PURSE. Its first recorded use in a sexual sense is in the C17 in a Beaumont and Fletcher play.

PUSS. From the C17 onwards this has been a popular word; pussy, however, is a newcomer and only appeared in the C20. As well as the cat, **puss** was the name for the hare, another animal associated with the night, soft fur and fertility. In the Middle Ages the hare was called the bromkat, the cat of the woods. Hares were believed to change sex each spring, being male one year and female the next.

QUAINT. Slang that goes back to the C16 and stayed the course until the C19. The spelling 'queynte' is also occasionally seen and both may be unskilled attempts to spell **cunt**.

QUARRY. An ambiguous word; does it mean a huntsman's prey or a place where rocks are cut from the earth? Either could be appropriate but perhaps the idea of a pit or hole is intended in this C18 slang.

QUID. Although this may sound like slang for £1, it is actually Latin for the question 'what?'. The Romans did not use the word as slang for the pudenda, preferring *illa* (meaning 'that'). (see Chapter 8.)

QUIFF. This is an example of back-formation in slang, the word being derived from 'quiffing', meaning intercourse.

QUIM. From the Welsh word *cwm* meaning a valley. First appearing in the C17, **quim** is still heard; it was the favourite name in the rugger songs I learned – along with passing, drop-kicking and tackling – in the 1960s. **Quim** variations include quim-box, quem, quimsby and queme.

QUONIAM. Latin for 'whereas' and slang for the **punse** from the C14 to the C18.

RASP. A painful-sounding C19 expression. (See Chapter 5 for information on rasping.)

RATTLE-BOLLOCKS. Lively and vivid C18 slang, suggesting that a vigorous good time was had by somebody. A London court record from the C14 notes that a whore named Clarice la Clatterballock was arrested for plying her trade. What a pity 'clatterballocks' did not become part of the language.

REST AND BE THANKFUL. A pious-sounding sentiment found on the back of public benches and seats in the C19 and C20. These free seats were of obvious benefit and pleasure to mankind and I shall say no more on the matter.

RING. A description that goes back to ancient Roman times and probably even farther. These days the word is more often used to mean the anus.

ROAD. Goes back to the C17 and is more euphemistic than slang, perhaps. A longer version is the phrase 'road to a christening'.

ROB-THE-RUFFIAN. Presumably the ruffian has his potency drained away during sex. This is another C19 usage that reveals male anxieties.

ROOSTER. Where the **cock** rested in the mid-C19.

ROSE. Generally a term for a maidenhead, **rose** was used by Shakespeare but does not seem to have become a popular piece of slang until the mid-C18.

ROUGH-AND-TUMBLE. Dating from about 1850, **rough-and-tumble**, together with the terms 'rough-and-ready' and 'rough-o', are extensions of the idea of a woman as 'a bit of rough'.

RUFUS. Pubic hair of any colour, according to C19 slang.

SADDLE. The word was applied both to the sex organ and to women in general and came into use in the C17, though it has been rare since 1750.

SALT-CELLAR. Linked to **salt**, meaning copulation, and to the idea of salt as something precious, this was popular in the C19 but is no longer heard.

SCRUBBING BRUSH. Coined in the mid-C19, when cleanliness was next to godliness and all minds were pure.

SEMINARY. This laboured pun on semen was the 1850s idea of a joke.

SHAKE-BAG. To C18 slang users this meant a prostitute; to those in the following century a **cunt**.

SHARP AND BLUNT. A specimen of oxymoronic rhyming slang cooked up in the London of the 1890s.

SHEATH. Not so much slang as a direct translation of the Latin *vagina*, though the coiner may not have realised it. Other martial containers in use are the quiver and scabbard.

SHOOTER'S HILL. A pun on the name of a London district that first appeared in the C19.

SILENT BEARD, SILENT HAIR. A brace of C19 expressions for pubic hair.

SIR BERKELEY, SIR BERKELEY HUNT, LADY BERKELEY, BERK. Basic rhyming slang dating from the 1880s; **berk** is still in regular use and many people have no idea what it means.

SKIN COAT. One more credited to Sir Thomas Urquhart in the 1650s. Coition is to 'shake a skin coat'.

SLIT. A word that has been part of slang since the C18 and, because of its physical accuracy, has come close to achieving respectability. But only close, so far.

SLUICE. A moist name in use from the C17 until early in the C20.

SNATCH, SNATCH-BLATCH. Yorkshire dialect is the original home of this expression, which crossed to the USA and made itself at home there. Before the current meaning came into being during the late C19, a **snatch** meant a quickie. Or, in the sonorous words of Eric Partridge, 'a hasty or illicit or mercenary copulation'.

> There once was a young girl named Jeanie
> Whose dad was a terrible meanie:
> He fashioned a latch
> And hatch for her snatch –
> She could only be had by Houdini.

SNIPPET. A name used in Liverpool about a century ago but no longer understood, according to my personal research in the 1990s.

SOUTH POLE. The century before last was a golden age of exploration and a suitable seedbed for this metaphor.

SPLEUCHAN. A nice, moist-sounding word that you can find in *The Merry Muses of Caledonia* by Burns.

South Pole

SPLIT. An uninspired anatomical description, in print from 1850 or so, but even older in speech: 'I felt it, the dear little split – how I wish my belly had been up against it!' said a lecher of the day.

SPORTSMAN'S GAP, SPORTSMAN'S HOLE. According to one expert, this blends the huntsman's very welcome gap in a hedge with the idea of the sporting house or brothel.

STANDING ROOM FOR ONE. An omnibus conductor's cry from 1840 put to a fresh use in this slang.

STREAM'S TOWN. Often abbreviated to 's.t.', the expression was in use during the period 1820–70.

SUGAR BASIN, SUGAR BOWL. Forerunners in the C19 of modern endearments such as 'sweetie', 'sugar', 'honey', etc.

TAIL. An ancient description, dating back to circa 1350, and considered perfectly decent until the C18; then it slipped several rungs down the respectability ladder. **Tail** emigrated to America and became very successful, and in recent times it has reappeared in the UK.

The word was used in combination to create a number of other sexual terms, for example: tail fruit (children); tail feathers (pubic hair); tail-fence (the hymen) and hot-tailed (suffering from VD).

TEMPLE OF THE LOW MEN. Punning on the Temple of Hymen and considered too utterly witty in the 1890s. Hymen was, of course, the personification of the god of marriage. In Classical Greek *humen* meant a membrane, such as the thin one found partially blocking the vagina. An unbroken hymen was evidence of virginity and rupturing it an act prized by many men. In physiological terms the hymen has no useful purpose.

TENCH. A most unkind comparison; the tench is a freshwater fish notable for being covered in thick slime and tasting of mud. Perhaps it is a misprint for 'trench', which isn't much kinder.

In parts of France the tench is stuffed with mushroom, bay, breadcrumbs, hard-boiled egg and parsley before being slowly baked in white wine. But it still tastes of mud.

TETBURY PORTION. A mixed blessing from the Cotswold market town, since the portion was defined from 1780–1860 as 'a cunt and the clap'.

THAT. Not really slang but a Victorian way of avoiding say some dreadful word that might cause God to smite your foul tongue with lightning. The Romans used the same euphemism (see **illa** in Chapter 8).

THATCHED HOUSE UNDER THE HILL. Popular from circa 1770–1850 and another of the rural metaphors slang loves. Later on it was shortened to 'the house under the hill'; the artist Aubrey Beardsley wrote an erotic novel entitled *Under the Hill*

THING, THINGAMY, THINGUMABOB, THINGUMAJIG. All C19 and all showing slang as a veil draped across what contemporary society considers *nasty*.

TICKLE THOMAS. Another C19 example; the Thomas in question must be that fine, upstanding chap **John Thomas** (see Chapter 3). A broadside ballad of the 1650s called 'A Westminster Wedding, or Like unto Like, quoth the Devil to the Collier' has a chorus that runs:

> Tom come tickle me, Tom come tickle me,
> Tom come tickle me over again.

Whether that influenced the slang or was based on the slang I do not know.

TILL. As in the place where cash is kept rather than 'Till we meet again'; the wealth-obsessed C19 provided this.

TIRLY-WIRLY. One from C18 Scotland and used by the poet Burns in one of his saucy moments.

TIVY, TIVVY. A word that may be drawn from the C19 country dialect word 'tivey', meaning active.

TOUCH-HOLE. An offering from the C17 arms trade; on muskets and pistols the touch-hole was the gunpowder vent in a firearm where a small charge was placed to ignite the main one in the barrel.

TREASURE OF LOVE. Introduced to the public by Cleland in *Fanny Hill* in 1749.

TUZZYMUZZY. Recorded in 1710 and taken from a dialect word meaning a posy of flowers or a nosegay. In the early C19 a publisher called William Dugdale put out a songbook called *The Tuzzymuzzy Songster*

TWAT. Derived from the dialect *twachylle*, meaning passage and *twatch* (to block a hedge gap), **twat** caused one of the Glorious Blunders of English Literature. The Victorian poet Robert Browning believed **twat** was part of a nun's costume and mentioned it in a poem 'Pippa Passes':

> Then, owls and bats,
> Cowls and twats,
> Monks and nuns in cloister's moods,
> Adjourn to the oak-stump pantry.

His mistake was due to an innocent reading of Fletcher's 1660 translation of the Roman poet Martial's 'Vanity of Vanities':

> They talk't him having a Cardinalls Hat,
> They'd send him as soon an Old Nuns Twat.

No one could be found with enough courage to inform Browning of his mistake. Related terms include twat-rug (pubic hair), twat-masher (a lover) and twat-faker or pimp, as we prefer these days.

UNDER-BELONGINGS, UNDER-DIMPLE, UNDER-ENTRANCE, UNDERWORLD. Basic locational slang coming into use in the C19.

VALVE. There is a strong suspicion that this late-C19 effort is not so much slang as a mishearing of the medical term vulva.

VENERABLE MONOSYLLABLE. A long-winded version of **monosyllable** used from 1780–1840 and occasionally revived in a joking (I hope) fashion.

VENUS'S HONEYPOT. As you would expect, there are plenty of expressions featuring the Goddess of Love; this one is from the C18. Other terms are Venus's glove, Venus's highway, Venus's mark and Venus's secret cell. These were in use from the C17 to the C20 and could stand reviving.

> There was a young fellow called Bliss
> Whose sex-life was sadly amiss
> For, when summoned by Venus,
> His recalcitrant penis,
> Could never do better than t
>   h
>   i
>   s

Whelk

WATER-MILL. Another grinding image from the C19. Other soggy expressions include waterbox, watercourse and water-gap.

WHELK. One more variety of shellfish added to the menu, to go with the **oyster** and **periwinkle**. This specimen arrived in 1860 and featured in the Cockney catch phrase 'I'll 'ave yer whelk.'

WHERE UNCLE'S DOODLE GOES. A C19 phrase warning that relatives were not to be trusted.

WHETTING-CORNE. In the C17 this meant a grindstone. Whetstone itself did not become a slang term but 'whetstone mutton' meant a whore in the C16.

WORST PART. An unkind and cheap name for a place where the man who invented it probably liked to park his **tarse**.

3. FINE, UPSTANDING CHAPS

There are fewer slang terms for the male equipment than for the female; either nobody could be bothered to invent more or the subject offers less scope for the imagination. The predominant image is of the erect, firm organ (a **bit of hard**), deserving admiration and ready to satisfy a woman's wildest cravings. Occasionally it may be admitted, shyly, that the tower-power has problems, frequently alcohol-related, i.e. 'brewer's droop'. (If you're a size-worrier you can add to your uncertainties by fretting about number, as well, since zoologists have discovered that Komodo dragons, koalas and iguanas all have two penises.)

The commonest names heard in the UK are also some of the oldest. **Tool** first came to hand in 1252; **cock** strutted into the henhouse about 1400 and **prick** was recorded in 1592. Other, older terms existed, like **tarse** (from the eleventh century, the same vintage as **limb** and **weapon**), and **yard**, noted in 1379 and active until the 1800s. **Weapon** is still heard in the sexual sense, though **tarse** shrivelled away long ago.

Images of weapons that stab, shoot or batter are standard usage when slang describes the penis; the words often seem intended to impress and awe other males rather than have any appeal to women. Occasionally less butch terms saunter into the language, like **lollipop** and **tit-bit**, but they tend not to linger. Male employment gives rise to some slang, such as **gardener** and **customs officer**. The meat trade serves up a number of dishes, including **butcher**, **beef** and **chitterling**, not forgetting **meat** itself.

Personal names have proved popular over the centuries, **John Thomas** and **Man John**, **Jacob**, **Julius Caesar**, **Captain Standish** and **Sir Martin Wagstaff**, and **Nimrod**, **Old Rowley**, **Peter** and **Willy** are also to be found in the congregation.

There are the odd names taken from dialects and jargons, such as **bingey**, **bracmard**, **dowsetts**, **pecnoster** and **tooleywag**. Rhyming slang gives a number of expressions, such as **almond rock** and **Pat and Mick**.

Read on and be amazed, or at least amused.

AARON'S ROD. A biblical reference from the C19; in *Hebrews*, chapter 9, verse 4, we learn that Aaron's rod had buds, i.e. children. Aaron's rod is also the dialect name for various wild flowers, like agrimony, golden rod and mullein.

ADAM'S ARSENAL. Adam is in the Bible but there are no chapter and verse references to his arsenal. The name has given rise to poetry, including the short verse in English: 'Adam/Had 'em', allegedly referring to fleas. I think a more likely explanation is this:

> In the Garden of Eden lay Adam,
> Complacently stroking his madam,
> And loud was his mirth
> For he knew that on Earth
> There were only two balls – and he had 'em.

One of the weapons in the arsenal was 'Adam's dagger' but the blade bust in the late C18 and nobody bothered to mend it.

AFFAIR. Literary and in use during the last quarter of the C19; in the tale *Sub-Umbra, or Sport Among the She-Noodles* you can find: 'I had placed one hand under her buttocks, whilst, with the other, I kept my affair straight to the mark.'

Sizism as a prejudice where **affairs** are concerned can be observed in the following sad verse:

> A nudist resort in Benares
> Took a midget in all unawares
> But he made members weep
> For he just couldn't keep
> His nose out of private affairs.

ALMOND ROCK. Rhyming slang dating back to 1840–50 and often shortened to **almond**.

ARBOR VITAE. Latin for 'tree of life', used from the C18 by pedants, dreary ushers and other academic show-offs. The female equivalent is **frutex vulvaria**.

ARROW. One of the C19 weapon-based pieces of slang that were popular in the porn of the day; there is something from *The Pearl* of 1880:

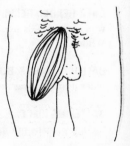

Almond Rock

What an indescribable heat reigned in the luscious folds of her
cunt! Ye Gods! How often did I dart my stiffened arrow through
the rich, juicy flesh of her deliciously sensitive quiver.

ARSE-SPLITTER, ARSE WEDGE. Aggressive Victorian language suggesting either
sodomy by intent or a crap sense of direction.

BABY-MAKER. Proof that one slangmaker understood the basics of the human
reproductive system. This is more euphemism than slang, however, and was
introduced in the late C19.

BACON. In the 1920s and 1930s this was slang for the **cock**.

BAG AND STONES. The scrotum (dear old wrinkled retainer) and testicles, a
slightly literary image from about 1870. The athletic hero of the 1880 novella *La
Rose d'Amour* recalled a merry romp with several girls:

> Oh! Then what amorous, wanton tricks we sportively played each
> other, they tickling my large bags and stones, playing with my
> penis and rubbing it, I moulding their beautiful titties and with the
> tip of my finger tickling their cunts.

Bags? How well endowed the fellow was.

BAG OF TRICKS. The conjurer's full set in the slang of around 1850.

BALD-HEADED HERMIT. Partridge calls this C19 phrase 'cultured', so perhaps the
wits of the 1890s used it. Can you imagine this dropping from the lips of Oscar
Wilde?

BALLOCKS, BALLS, BOLLOCKS. The testicles in C19 slang. **Ballocks** is a much
older term and was acceptable speech until the early C19.

BATTERING PIECE. Presumably on the lines of a battering ram but smaller –
though perhaps not in the eye of the C17 owner.

BAYONET. Cuts into sex slang during the 1840s; when it is a 'fixed bayonet' the penis is erect and ready to go over the top. Beef bayonet is a later fleshy blade.

BEAK. This is seldom used except in **strop your beak**, one of the C19 phrases for intercourse. The word has other slang meanings, like schoolmaster, magistrate and even, on rare occasions, policeman.

BEARD-SPLITTER. In the C18 pubic hair was called the **beard**, hence this image.

BEEF. A meaty image for the penis that was first recorded early in the C19 and is still heard today.

BELLY-RUFFIAN. A coarse but graphic piece of language that enjoyed popularity from the C17 to the C19.

BILLY. The word could be drawing on the idea of a truncheon or club, called a billy in C19 criminal slang, or a rustic memory of a billy goat and his activities, or even a billycock/billycoke hat, now better known as the bowler hat.

Beef

BINGEY. A sample of nursery slang from the 1890s; it is Anglo-Irish and based on a dialect word for hitting, 'bing'.

BIT OF HARD. An erect penis according to late-C19 and C20 slang.

BLACKPOOL ROCK. Rhyming slang and possibly concocted in the 1920s and 1930s when George Formby Jr sang the ditty 'With Me Little Stick of Blackpool Rock'.

BLIND. An uncircumcised penis of 1920s vintage.

BLUEBEARD. This name is based on the murderous husband Bluebeard in a fairy story; it was also the nickname of the French killer Landrau. It is no longer used much.

BLUE VEIN. An erect penis in slang dating from 1910. The nickname was very popular in America in the 1960s and 1970s and inspired the following joke in the UK at around the same time: What is about five inches long, has a blue vein running down it, and girls love to hold it? A five-pound note.

BODKIN. A sharp tool for pricking holes or a short dagger, perhaps taken from the Welsh *bidog*, meaning dagger. Used in sexual slang for about two centuries from the C17.

BONE. A C19 **hard on**.

BOW. In 1800 this was used to play the female **fiddle**. It may also have meant the weapon for shooting Cupid's arrows.

BOWSPRIT. A nautical word that came to anchor about 1750 then sailed on into the mists of forgotten words.

BOYO. A jocular personification of the **yard** from the C19.

BRACMARD. A *braquemard* was a short French sword used in the C17; the English contraction entered slang in that century but it has not been used much since.

BRAT-GETTER. The practical view of the male organ, popular in the C19.

BRIDLE-STRING. An item of tack that riders might not find in the stables, except on the stable-lad, of course.

BRITANNIA METAL. An erection in C19 UK slang; the original metal was an alloy rather like pewter.

BROOM-HANDLE. The stiffie in a domestic setting, just waiting for the firm grip of the housewife. When I first met this slang I thought of witches astride their flying brooms, not the homely device kept in the special cupboard.

BUM-BALLS. The testicles in mid-C19 argot.

BUNGLER. An impotent man in terminology popular in the years 1660–1720.

BUSH-BEATER. Either what the sadistic forester gets up to in his spare time or another C19 word meaning the **cock**.

BUTCHER. A master tradesman doing duty in the C19 for the **member**.

BUTTER KNIFE. The butter in question is semen and the term appears to have enjoyed a brief career in public life in the C19.

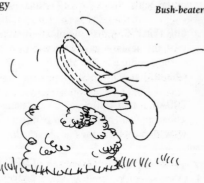

Bush-beater

CALLIBISTERS. A C16 name for the testicles that is somehow pleasingly round and cheerful.

CANNONBALLS. Martial C19 slang for the **goolies**.

CAPTAIN STANDISH. A military man, always standing to attention and always ready for action. The gallant officer first paraded in the 1730s.

CASTOR AND POLLUX. A C19 slangmonger with classical learning applied the names of the Gemini twins to his nuts.

CATSO. Developed from the Italian word *cazzo* (penis), this term pleased slang-speakers from 1660 or so until the early C18. It also meant a rogue or villain.

CAVALIER. Schoolboys soon learn if they are **cavaliers** (intact and uncircumcised) or the opposite: **roundheads**. The slang began in schools in the C19.

CHERRY-SPLITTER. A cherry was a young girl in dialect; the idea of a cherry being a maidenhead is based on that but it is an American term rather than British, though it has become increasingly popular in the UK in the last 25 years

CHILD-GETTER. One of the rare pieces of slang pointing out the procreative use of the penis. From the C19 and cousin to **brat-getter**.

CHITTERLING. A dish of animal intestines chopped up and cooked. Also, in the C19, the penis. A gaudier version was 'crimson chitterling'. Some scenes in the pornographic tale *The Modern Eveline* are set in a country house named Chitterlings.

CHOAD. A mid-C20 name for the penis that seems only to exist in the form 'choadsmoker', anyone who performs fellatio. It has been suggested that the word derives from the Navaho *chodis*, meaning penis.

Clothes-prop

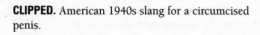

CLIPPED. American 1940s slang for a circumcised penis.

CLOTHES-PROP. Another domestic image and popular in the C19. Now that most people own washing machines and tumble driers, do they know what a clothes-prop is?

CLUB. A piece of weapon-based slang from the C18–C19. This is not the club that pregnant women are said to be in, which is the Pudding Club.

COBBLERS, COBBLER'S AWLS. The balls in C19 rhyming slang.

COBS. As in cobnuts – slang for the balls from 1830 or so.

COCK. Already discussed in some detail, this has been with us since 1400 and shows no sign of shrinking away. If it was good enough for Shakespeare to use, it's good enough for the rest of us. 'Cockstand' was C18 slang for an erection.

COD, CODS. The singular is the scrotum, the plural is the testicles. Both terms became popular in the C19, but are older.

COLLEEN BAWN. Rhyming slang for **horn**; the Irish words literally mean 'the fair girl' as in the 1860 Boucicault play of that title.

CONCERN. Like **affair** and **private parts** this is a semi-genteel expression and was most popular in the 1840s.

COPPER-STICK. After the stick used to stir the contents of the copper, a large cauldron used for laundry, and from the C18. Or it is from the truncheon carried by policemen? Take your pick.

CORAL BRANCH. A C19 comment on the pink or red shade of the member and perhaps its hardness.

CRACK HUNTER. The penis as predator – a C19 vision of male lust on the prowl.

CRACKSMAN. In 1810 this was applied to a housebreaker; in 1850 the sexual meaning came into fashion.

CREAM STICK. Unsubtle but exact, **cream stick** was used in the C18; the word 'cream' meaning semen on its own was not served up until the following century.

CREDENTIALS. A description of the penis and testicles from 1895.

CUCKOO. Not a piece of Merrie England rural picturesque dialect, but urban schoolboys' slang from the late C19.

CUCUMBER. This became popular in the C19, when Victorian gardeners enclosed the fruit in glass tubes to make them as straight as possible. The Roman emperor Tiberius had his cucumbers grown in wheelbarrows so that they could be moved into the sun.

CULLIONS, CULLS. The testicles (a word that means 'little witnesses') and used in the C17 by Shakespeare's oppo Ben Jonson. But another poet, long before Jonson, had used the word, though with his own spelling: Chaucer. In *The Canterbury Tales* the Host teases the eunuch-like Pardoner, saying:

> I wolde I hadde thy coillions in myn honed …
> They shud be shryned in an hogges toord.

Holding a pair of balls coated in pig shit may have been entertainment in the Middle Ages but I can't see it catching on again. We're just not sophisticated enough.

CULTY GUN. This combines two weapons, which is plain greedy. **Culty** is short for **cutlass**.

CUNT RAMMER. Chiefly a pornographer's image from the 1860s to the 1890s. Typically Walter was familiar with the slang: 'She walked to the door, but looked at my cunt rammer long, and laughed before she went: I felt sure I had made her lewd.'

CUPID'S BATTERING RAM. A metaphor from the 1870s and 1880s, found in our friend *The Pearl*, e.g. 'The red head of "Cupid's Battering Ram" was now brought to the charge ...' etc., etc.

CUSTOMS OFFICER. The official responsible for controlling **Eve's custom-house** – see Chapter 2.

CUTLASS. The short, heavy sword that was used by the Royal Navy and pirates to reduce opponents to the consistency of chopped liver. Exactly the image needed for the penis.

> There was a young pirate named Bates
> Who danced the fandango on skates,
> But a fall on his cutlass
> Rendered him nutless
> And practically useless on dates.

DAGGER. Simple weapon slang put into print in the C18 but probably in spoken use long before that.

DANGLERS. Basic C19 terminology for those not bright enough to use **Castor and Pollux**.

DART, DART OF LOVE, LOVE-DART. Based on the image of the arrow and throwing dart the terms appear in the C18; **Cupid's dart** and **dart of love** were still popular at the end of the C19.

'There, Annie, take the dart of love in your hand.' She grasped it nervously, as she softly murmured: 'Oh, Walter, I'm so afraid; and yet – oh, dearest, I feel, I die, I must taste the sweets of love, this forbidden fruit.'

Dart

Ah, they don't write 'em like that anymore. This scene from *Sub-Umbra* features lecherous Walter seducing one of his cousins.

DEAD RABBIT. Not a poacher's delight on a shiny night, but a flaccid penis.

DERRICK. A rather sinister name for the penis; a **derrick** is a crane, but originally was a gallows, devised by the public hangman, Derrick, in the early C17.

DICK. Along with **cock**, **prick** and **tool**, a major slang term. Originally it was a military term used from circa 1860 and becoming popular outside the Army from about 1880 onwards. It may have started life in the phrase 'Tom, Dick and Harry'. Like **prick** it has morphed into a variety of forms, e.g. dickhead. Dicky is a version sometimes used by children. NB: the phrase 'swallow the dick' does not mean what you're thinking, but to use very long words as a consequence of having swallowed the dic(tionary).

DIDDLER. Slang for a small member, in use in the early C19. Probably not much in use if it was really small.

DING-DONG, DONG. These started life in the C19 and, in the case of **dong** especially, are still alive and swinging.

DINGBAT. In some parts of the world during the early decades of the C20 this meant the penis; in Australia and New Zealand it meant somebody was insane.

DIRK. The Scottish version of **dagger**, in use from 1600 onwards.

DOMINIE DO-LITTLE. A man afflicted with a **dead rabbit** in this late-C18 phrase. **Dominie** being a term for a schoolmaster north of the border, the slang may be Scottish.

DON CYPRIANO. One of the many literary names for the **cock** thought up by Sir Thomas Urquhart in the 1650s. A Cyprian was a whore, named after Cyprus where Aphrodite, the goddess of love, was born.

DONKEY DICK, DONKEY RIG. A notably large organ, often with a small brain in charge of it.

DOODLE. A spineless-sounding term from the latter part of the C19. Walter made use of the word from time to time, e.g. His doodle had stood, but drooped directly her lips left it. Sometimes expanded (with luck) to doodle-pipe.

DOWSETTS. In the hunting terminology of the C17 these were a stag's testicles – and considered good eating.

DR JOHNSON. After the pugnacious dictionary-maker, who would stand up to anyone; this piece of slang was in use from 1780–1880.

DRUMSTICK. The leg of a fowl or the musicmaker's tool; which is meant by this C19 name? The plural form does not mean two pricks but the legs.

ENGINE. John Cleland gave this word its sexual energy in *Fanny Hill*, published in 1749. It was still popular with pornographers in the 1880s in the form 'engine of love'. Again *The Pearl* can provide a short example: 'I felt her dear lips again pressing and sucking my engine of love.'

EQUIPMENT. The Full Monty of penis and testicles in C19 slang. Excessive size may cause problems:

> There was a young man of Coblentz
> Whose equipment was simply immense,
> It took forty-four draymen,
> A priest and three laymen
> To carry it thither and thence.

EYE-OPENER. Does this C19 slang commemorate an organ so splendid that female eyes opened wide in amazement? Or did the eyes open wide in an attempt to spot the thing at all? Might, perhaps, the eye be a reference to the vagina?

FAMILY JEWELS. The testicles, according to C19 slang; they were sometimes downgraded by being spoken of as mere **trinkets**. In the 1960s family jewels reappeared, this time meaning the full set of genitals.

FATHER ABRAHAM. A name used in the C19 and based on the idea of the biblical Abraham being the father of his people. The female equivalent was 'Abraham's bosom'.

FERRET. One more in the menagerie of creatures that spend much of their careers down holes; the verb is ferreting.

FLAPDOODLE. A piece of C17 slang; as well as the penis, the word could mean a hobbyhorse.

FLAPPER. This conjures up an image of a 1920s babe, with bandeau, beaded skirt, long cigarette-holder and an insatiable desire to Charleston. Sadly, it was a C19 word for a limp **dick**.

FLESH FLUTE. Played from the early part of the last century.

FLOWERS AND FROLICS. More C19 poetic argot for the **goolies**.

FOOL-MAKER, FOOLSTICK. Either the owner of the item is making a fool of some husband by having his wife, or else only fools propagate the species and their offspring are fools, too. You pays your money and you takes your choice in this C19 slang.

Flesh Flute

FORNICATOR. The organ and its owner in the C19 but the word was/is Standard English. Other expressions were fornicating engine and fornicating tool and these can be considered genuine slang because of the second word in each phrase.

FUCK-BEGGAR. A man who was poverty-stricken when it came to copulation, i.e. incapable whether sober or drunk. The name dates from the C18.

FUCKSTICK. Direct, unadorned slang from the C19.

FUMBLER. From the end of the C17 until the middle of the C18 a **fumbler** was an impotent man. His address was given as **Fumbler's Hall** (see Chapter 2).

GADSO. A variant of **catso**.

GARDEN ENGINE, GARDENER. Linked, naturally enough, with **garden** equating to vagina, but not dating back to the C16 like that expression. These are early-C19 additions to the sexual lexicon.

GAYING INSTRUMENT. From the early part of the C19 when **gaying** meant sexual intercourse.

GEAR. An example of a standard term without any low or criminal connections minding its own business from the C16 and being used by people without a care, until, wham, the Victorian prudes (whose minds were the dirtiest about) decided that **gear** was vulgar, obscene and unsavoury. However, you can't keep a good word down and **gear** is still tripping off tongues all over the UK.

GENIALS. A clever play on genitals from the 1850s.

GENTLEMAN USHER. The penis as an official, according to the slang of the late C16 and early C17.

GIRL-CATCHER. In 1870 this was considered an awfully jolly, jaunty way to describe the good old **engine**.

GIRLOMETER. A modern-sounding word that actually dates from 1870.

GHOOLIES, GOOLIES. Some experts say this comes from gully, an old word for a marble, and others claim it comes from the Hindustani *gola* meaning ball. The word has been in English slang since about 1885.

GOSPEL PIPE. An expression from the US of A and dating to 1910.

HAMPTON. Rhyming slang of the late C19; Hampton Wick – **prick**. Easy-peasy, right?

HANDSTAFF. An agricultural image, naming the handle of a flail, this slang came into use in the early part of the C19.

HANGING JOHNNY. A double misfortune, because not only is the organ as limp as Long John Silver, it also has VD.

HARD ON. An erection in UK and US slang.

HOG. The word is correctly applied to a castrated boar, but some creative thinker in the C19 either didn't know or didn't care.

HOG LEG. At first this American slang was applied to the Colt .45 revolver but before long the name took a dive into a cowboy's chaps and attached itself to the penis.

HORN. An erection described by slang going back into the Dark Ages of language. It was written down in the C17 but the oral tradition of folksong is far older. 'Horn colic' meant an involuntary erection and was part of English slang from 1750 to 1900.

HOT LOT. The penis in American slang of the early C20; the term 'hot member' was also popular at that time and in that place.

IMPUDENCE. Rather coy slang for the **tarse** employed from about 1750–1870.

INSTRUMENT. A curiosity, this one; I have seen references to it as slang for the penis but cannot find an example of it except in the compound **gaying instrument**.

IRISH HORSE. The impotent penis in C19 language.

IRISH ROOT. An expression that was part of English slang from 1830–1914, a period when the Irish were regarded half the time as comical serfs and the other half as dangerous rebels. Sometimes slang mentions an 'Irish toothache', meaning either an erection or pregnancy.

JACK ROBINSON. The penis as a person; see also **John Thomas**, **John Willie** and **Man John**. The name is C19 slang.

JACOB. One more example of naming slang, drawing on the Bible.

JARGONELLE. A fruity comparison from 1750s, the name being that of a variety of pear. In France the same fruit is called *Cuisse Madame*, meaning lady's thigh.

JIGGER, JIGGLING BONE. The first word can also mean the vagina and a lock. The second term is an elaboration of the first and both were used in the C19.

JOCK. This is a contraction of **jockum**, a mid-C16 name for the male organ, which originally had a feminine meaning (see Chapter 2). The expressions **jock** and **jockum-cloy** both mean sexual intercourse. **Jock** has survived into the C21, chiefly in schoolboy slang and as the supportive **jockstrap**.

JOHN THOMAS. Originally a name applied to any male servant – as Mary Anne and Mary Jane were to females – but in the 1850s the penis was baptised **John Thomas**. Why? Because a flunky always stood when ladies were present.

John Thomas

JOHN WILLIE. He started life in a Lancashire catch phrase 'John Willie, come on!', which was shouted at slow-witted men to encourage thought. A music-hall song performed by George Formby Sr circa 1910 related the mildly saucy adventures of John Willie, whose wife was always urging him to 'Come on'.

JOHNSON. This mid-C19 name may be a shortening of **Dr Johnson** in British use. In the USA it is almost certainly taken from the champion boxer Jack Johnson. The slang appears to be in use again in the UK as an American import.

JOINT. Not an exotic smoke but either: a) a method of fixing together two pieces of wood; or, b) an item found in the **butcher's shop** (see Chapter 2).

JULIUS CAESAR. Along with weapons and tools, C19 slangmongers were keen on names; here is another one, dating from 1840 or so. Who knows why a long-dead bisexual, bald Roman politico suddenly appealed?

JUMBLE-GIBLETS. A muddled-up-sounding name for the **yard** used in the C17.

KENNEL RAKER. Unsavoury image of the **tool** employed in the C19.

KIDNEY-WIPER. A large **cock** in the slang of 1850 and again in the 1960s, when the expression emerged from the undergrowth and reintroduced itself.

KIT. The full set: penis and testicles. **Kit** first came into popular use in the 1850s and may come from the full kit possessed by sailors and soldiers, which was inspected at regular intervals.

KNOCK, KNOCKER. From the C18 to the C20, the penis as an item of door furniture.

LADIES' DELIGHT, LADIES' TREASURE. Two optimistic phrases from the 1850s.

LANCE. From the C19, when themes from the days of chivalry were popular and light cavalry regiments called Lancers still carried eight-foot bamboo spears. 'Lance in rest' indicated that the owner had the **horn**.

LANGOLEE. Learned men think this slang is a mangling of a Welsh gypsy word, *trangluni*, meaning tools.

LEATHER STRETCHER. Slang that enjoyed a 200-year reign from the C18 to the C20. The **leather** being stretched was female, of course. 'Leather dresser' is a similar name from the same period.

LIFE PRESERVER. Meaning a cosh or blackjack, and drawing attention to the likeness between cosh and **cock** in the C19.

LIMB. Like **member** this is not so much slang as euphemism. It has been more often used to describe a child. It was first used in the sexual sense in the C11 but had turned respectable, though very slowly, passing away about 1900.

LITTLE BROTHER. The sibling to **little sister** (met in Chapter 2), he was also born around 1850.

LITTLE DAVEY. A modest man, stepping shyly into the language in the C19.

LIVE RABBIT. A phrase applied to both the penis and a prostitute circa 1840.

LIVER-LIFTER. A promising description of a **pego**, which came into the language in the first half of the C19.

LOB, LAZY LOB. A partial erection, coined from a C16 word for droop.

LOBCOCK. In the C18 this meant a large, floppy **tool**.

LOLLIPOP. Infrequently used word (in this context) that had a sexual meaning applied to it in the C19.

LONG TOM. A late-C19 boast about the **pego**.

LORD KNOWS WHAT. Bewilderment crying out in the C17. A polite expression rather than street slang, perhaps.

LOVE APPLES. Tender fruitiness in this C19 term for the **bollocks**.

LULLABY. Another uncommon term employed by some from 1850–1914. The idea was that the organ could put a woman to sleep, though whether from exhaustion or boredom was not made clear.

MACHINE. Apparently this C19 slang is based on the French word *machin*, which is equivalent to thingamajig, wotsisname, etc. During the C18 **machine** meant a condom.

In *La Rose d'Amour, or The Adventures of a Gentleman in Search of Pleasure* (1880), the hero makes boast with: 'My machine was proudly erect as a mast, its red head glowing through the darkness.'

Well, I suppose it saves buying torch batteries, but I'd run a Geiger counter over the thing just to be on the safe side.

MAD MICK. Australian rhyming slang from the middle of the last century.

MAGGOT. Like **worm** this cannot have been intended to flatter the penis or the attached owner.

MALE-MULES. An unflattering name for the testicles from the C16; since male mules are sterile, this must have been an insult.

MAN JOHN, MAN THOMAS. Simple naming slang, with the added nuances that **man** could mean a husband and sexual intercourse.

MARBLE HALLS. Rhyming slang for the **cods**, often shrunk to **marbles**.

MARQUIS OF LORNE. A peer whose title is a handy rhyme for **horn**.

MARROW PUDDING. The marrow is the tasty centre of a bone and not the pallid, watery vegetable whose looks are more promising than its taste.

MARROWBONE AND CLEAVER. Butchery as sex, the cleaver splitting open the bone to reach the soft, delicious marrow within. Work out the symbolic application for yourself.

MATRIMONIAL PEACEMAKER. Possibly optimistic notion from the C19.

MEAT. First served up as slang about 1620, the expression dropped out of use after two centuries but has enjoyed a revival in recent years.

MEAT AND TWO VEG. The penis and testicles put on the menu by slangmongers in the C19 and served up today.

MEMBER. Chaucer's lusty Wife of Bath talks of 'membres of generatioun', using a word that was part of the standard speech of the day and had been since the C13. Not until the C18 did the word move downmarket, supplying slangsters with clumsy puns like 'member for Cockshire'. Burns wrote of the 'dearest member' in 1740.

Mole

MERRYMAKER. Used for a **merry bout** (sex) with a merry legs (whore) and resulting in a merrybegot (bastard). These slang terms were found larking about from 1780–1830.

MOLE. Fat, furry and given to exploring tunnels; fine, we'll buy that. Eric Partridge describes this C19 word as 'low'. Where else would a mole be?

MORNING PRIDE. In the C19, as now, a chap could wake with a splendid 'fixed bayonet' only to discover that his **morning pride** was due to a full bladder rather than manly vigour. Also called pride of the morning.

MOWDIWARK. Scottish and North Country dialect of the C16 based on **mow**, meaning intercourse. Or perhaps the word is a lousy spelling of mouldiworp, an old country name for the mole.

MY BODY'S CAPTAIN. A distinctly poetic C19 way of indicating the **dick**. And poetic it should indeed sound, since the American writer Walt Whitman created the phrase.

NATURE'S SCYTHE. Some rural slangmaster of the early C19 thought this one up. Now that the scythe is rarely seen, the term has lost its cutting edge.

NEBUCHADNEZZAR. This biblical monarch (and very large champagne bottle) was sexually active from 1860 to the First World War. For those interested, a Nebuchadnezzar holds twenty normal bottles of champagne.

NEEDLE. In use during the C17, though the female **needlecase** arrived only in the C19. In 1664 the lecherous (and boastful) Earl of Dorset wrote the verse 'On Dolly Chamberlain, a Seamstress in the New Exchange':

> Dolly's Beauty and Art
> Have so hemm'd my Heart
> That I cannot resist her charm;
> In revenge I will stitch
> Up the hole next her breech
> With a needle as long as my arm.

See what I mean about boastful?

NICK-NACKS. The testicles were called by this name from 1750–1850.

NIGHT-STICK. Coined in the USA about 1900 and based on the long truncheon wielded by the police.

NIMROD. A biblical figure, the 'mighty hunter' mentioned in *Genesis*, chapter 10, verses 8–9. He was begat by Cush, if you're interested. Also the pen name of a great English writer about hunting, active around 1840–60. Oh, and slang for the **dick**.

NUTMEGS. A spicy name for the **bollocks** that was popular from the late C17 until 1850.

NUTS. This slang for the testicles first appeared in the C19 and is still used.

OLD ADAM. He makes his slang debut in the C19, but before that the name was Standard English for original sin.

OLD BLIND BOB. A sorry figure from the C18 slang dictionary; his one eye had failed him.

OLD HORNY, OLD HORNINGTON. Popular slang from the C18 onwards, with the ideas of horny (erection), Miss Horner (vagina) and Old Horney (the Devil) all rolled up into one phrase.

OLD MAN. An affectionate name, like **old lady**, dating from the middle part of the C19. If the **old man** 'had his Sunday clothes on', he was sporting an erection.

OLD ROWLEY. In the late C17 this meant the Devil or Charles II, whose interest in racing led to part of the Newmarket course being named 'the Rowley mile' – a measure of distance, not a personal best.

OLD SLIMEY. An unattractive **limb** hanging about the place in the C18.

ONE-EYED-BOY WITH HIS SLEEVES ROLLED UP. A late C19 description of a circumcised penis.

ONE-EYED STAG. From the late C18, an image suggesting deer stalking or going for tramps in the Highlands, e.g. 'Two Englishmen went for a tramp in the Highlands. They enjoyed it but the tramp wasn't too happy.'

PADDY'S TOOTHACHE. An erection.

PARTNER. Another simple, tender approach and apparently no longer used. The slang is from the C19, not generally an age noted for kindly images.

PAT AND MICK. This is an example of Anglo-Irish rhyming slang from 1890 or thereabouts.

PEBBLES. Did fond memories of seaside holidays inspire some slangmonger to thus name the testicles?

Pecker

PECKER. A confusing word, which can mean both the head and the appetite (for food) as well as the penis. All the meanings appear in the 1840s. The cheerful advice 'Keep your pecker up' was first issued in 1853. It still applies today.

The word is more often used in the USA and appears in songs such as 'The Woodpecker', sampled here:

> The woodpecker flew to the schoolhouse door
> And he pecked and he pecked until his pecker was sore.

PECNOSTER. A pun on paternoster (Our Father, i.e. the Lord's Prayer), which may have fathered **pecker**; it was first noted in the C19, which seems rather late for jokes about paternosters.

PEE-WEE. A C19 name for a small **tool**, probably American in origin.

PEGO. Once in widespread and regular use, this word, first recorded in 1709, is no longer heard. Some experts say it is taken from the Greek for a fountain, but a comparison with a tent peg, for example, seems more likely. **Peg** meaning intercourse does not arrive in slang until 1850.

The reliable *The Pearl* provides a great many examples of **pego** in use, including this from *La Rose d'Amour* in 1880: 'We kept glued together, till my pego drawing itself up into littleness, fell out from the juicy folds of its nest.'

PEN, PENCIL. Based on a pencil's shape and an abbreviation of penis, **pen** has been on active service since about 1550. A friend has told me that it was the first 'dirty word' she learned when she went to primary school in the 1960s and that her small son has picked it up in the same way in the 1990s. To 'have no ink in your pen' means to be impotent after too much sex. In the 1930s a **pencil** was a small penis.

While the shorter word does not seem to be honoured by any verses, **pencil** has this attached to it:

> There was a young man named Hentzel
> Blessed with a very long pencil,
> He went through an actress,
> Two sheets and a mattress,
> And shattered the family utensil.

PESTLE. As in 'pestle and mortar', the latter taking the female role in this C19 slang. The verb 'to pestle' means to fuck.

PETER. The naming of the male part, in line with **John Thomas, Captain Standish, Dr Johnson** et al.

PICKLE. A fairly recent addition to the list of penis names; however, as 'in pickle' (i.e. infected with clap or pox) the term dates back to the C17.

PIERCER. Rarely met slang that was around from 1840–70; it may well have been literary/pornographic rather than used in daily speech.

> With what delight I twiddled her cunt as we sat on the little sofa,
> where I had a glimpse of her garters, and naked thighs, and she
> bending her head, could see the florid knob of my piercer which
> she held in her hand.

That's our boy Walter, leading his secret life again.

PIKESTAFF. This is one of those hard, military comparisons that slang delights in. It was a cutting-edge expression in about 1705.

PILE-DRIVER. Neither imaginative nor, for the lady, comfortable. Thumping industrial slang from Victorian days.

PILGRIM'S STAFF. Before the Reformation the pilgrim plus his staff was a common sight and was certainly part of popular imagery. It seems odd that only in the C18, the Age of Enlightenment, was this slang created.

PILLOCKS, PILLS. Slang for the **callibisters** dating from the C19; the second word is a combination of **pills** and **ballocks**.

PINTLE. One of the most venerable names, going back to the Anglo-Saxon *pintel*, which was standard language and not slang. **Pintle** remained respectable, if common, until 1720, then began to be viewed as vulgar slang (except when it remained in dialects). Related terms are pintle-maid, meaning a mistress; pintle fever (VD) and **pintle-case**, vagina.

PIZZLE. This meant an animal's penis until the early C16 when a slangmaker transferred the sense to the human article. Tanned bull pizzles were often made into whips and criminals could be sentenced to a pizzling.

PLACKET-RACKET. An invention of our old friend Sir Thomas Urquhart's in the C17. Placket equals petticoat equals woman is combined with racket, as in tennis, that hits her.

PLENIPOTENTIARY. A name inspired by a dirty song of 1786, 'The Great Plenipotentiary'. The ditty appeared in a songbook by the music publisher William West with the title, The Blowen's Cabinet of choice songs: *A Beautiful, Bothering Laughter Provoking Collection of Spiflicating, Flabbergasting Smutty Ditties, Now First Printed, among Which Will Be Found The: Great Plenipotentiary!! A Most Outrageously Good Amatory Stave. Oh, Miss Tabitha Ticklecock!!!! A Slashing Smutty Ballad. The Magical Root or The Parslet Bed ...*

Plenipotentiary

This continues for another nine lines. A 'blowen', by the way, was a highwayman's mistress. West also published *The Cockchaser, The Gentleman's Spicy Songster* and *The Frisky Vocalist*, all crammed with good amatory staves, no doubt.

PLOUGHSHARE. An agricultural penis and an image that goes back to ancient Rome – (see Chapter 8).

PLUG-TAIL. A play on the female **tail** found in Ned Ward's 1699 book *A Walk to Islington*.

PLUM TREE SHAKER. A translation from the French *hoche-pannier* made by one Cotgrave in 1611.

POLE. The erect member described in stark and unambiguous language in the C19. James Joyce once contemplated writing a play featuring Baron Tostoff, a ruined Pole.

POLE-AXE. A long-handled halberd, a sailor's axe for chopping away damaged rigging and a tailor's axe-cum-hammer all offer origins for the slang. It could also mean the police in the C19.

POLYPHEMUS. The celebrated, one-eyed, cannibal giant of Homer's *Odyssey* bludgeoned his way into slang in the first half of the C19.

POTATO FINGER. In the C17 the same name was applied to the penis and a dildo; the second use was brought about by the belief that the sweet potato was an aphrodisiac and had a shape that seemed familiar.

PRICK. First noted in print in 1592 and nowadays perhaps the most-heard slang name. Partridge suggests it was once Standard English but the *OED* disagrees with him on that. Originally **prick** described C16 Jack-the-lads who were too sharp for their own good and that use does not seem to have had a sexual aspect. By 1680, when Lord Rochester was addressing poems to his **prick**, the slang was thoroughly at home. The following poem is not by his lordship:

> There was a young fellow of Kent
> Whose prick in the middle was bent;
> To save himself trouble,
> He put it in double
> And instead of coming he went.

PRIVATE PARTS. A humble soldier in the regiment of slang who made a modest entry in the C19, though 'privates' is much older; Shakespeare used it in *Hamlet*.

PUDDING. This is usually enjoyed by a woman as **hot pudding for supper**; a **pudding** can be **pulled** by a solitary sportsman. In either state it has been with us since 1685. (PS: it also means semen.)

PUMP. One from 1730 and most often encountered as 'pump ship', meaning to urinate.

PUTZ. A Yiddish word that is generally used as an insult and to indicate that the male possessing the **putz** is a klutz (a clumsy fool).

QUIMSTAKE, QUIMWEDGE. The masculine counterparts to the feminine **quim** and owing their existence to it. Both words go back to the C17; in current slang Quimwedge has been reduced to 'wedge'.

RAJAH. In 1940s New Zealand this was not an Indian prince but an erection.

RAMMER. This slang was more often used to indicate the arm, but in the mid-C19 it was sometimes applied to the penis. It was still in use in the late 1960s and early 1970s.

RAMROD. A stirring military description and enough to make any musketeer or gunner reach for his piece.

RANGER. The penis in the C17; a ranger's job was to patrol parkland and make sure poachers were kept at bay. At that time a woman's body was often compared to a park. In the C18 the word meant a wandering, inconstant sort of fellow; a promiscuous woman was sometimes indicated by the term pintle-ranger.

RANTALLION. The condition of having the scrotum drooping until it is longer than the penis, according to Grose in 1785. Try the term out in the squash club showers, chaps.

REAMER. I hope this does not refer to the spike-covered instrument that pipe-smokers clean their bowls with, but that hope may be in vain.

RED CAP. This does not mean the hallucinogenic fungus *Amanita muscaria* or a member of the Corps of Royal Military Police, but the **prick** – and the head in particular.

RHUBARB. The penis and testicles in common-or-garden slang of the late 1870s and 1880s.

ROARING JACK, ROARING HORN. An unusually raucous penis heard bawling in C19 Australia.

ROLLING PIN. Obviously based on the shape and optimistically on the size and rigidity. In *Lady Pockingham, or They All Do It* (published 1880) Mr William, the randy butler, chats to his **pintle** as he awaits the arrival of Lucy, the maid: 'Ah, I'm stiff as a rolling pin at the very thought of the saucy darling.'

ROLY-POLY. A name for a jam-sponge pudding in the 1840s and a **cock** four decades later.

ROOSTER. The penis, according to C19 Black American argot. The term appears in various C20 blues songs.

ROOT, THE OLD. Originally part of the biblical expression 'root of all evil', the abbreviation was used in the 1890s; it also meant an erection and money.

RUBIGO. Scottish slang from the C16; the word could be based on the Latin for red, *ruber*, or for rust, *robigo*, or the Latin *prurigo*, meaning lascivious. Nobody knows the truth.

RUMP-SPLITTER. Sir Thomas Urquhart's handiwork in 1650; does it indicate the **red cap's** use for sodomy?

SAM/SAMMY/SAMUEL HALLS. The balls, named after the anti-hero of a ballad of 1701. The man's name was actually Jack Hall and he was hanged for burglary. After death he underwent a change of name and became the singer of a sneering, gloating song, e.g:

> Oh, they say that I must die, I must die,
> They say that I must die, I must die,
> They say that I must die
> And they'll hang me up so high,
> Then I'll piss right in their eye, fuck 'em all.

British regiments under fire and waiting to charge the enemy often chanted the verses. Pious officers were shocked by it.

SAP. An old word for semen; 'spewing your sap' meant ejaculating.

SAUSAGE, LIVE SAUSAGE. On the menu from the 1890s and, in the view of some wise people, existing on the thin borderline between slang and colloquial speech.

SCEPTRE. No, not an essential item in a monarch's regalia, but the **tool** in the C19; the word is based on the Latin *sceptrum*, meaning a staff.

SEALS. Not aquatic mammals with a propensity for getting massacred while pups, but the kind of seal used to make a mark in hot sealing wax. Also an early-C19 term for the **nuts**.

SHAFT OF DELIGHT. An appreciative and cheery example of C18 slang.

SHLONG, SCHLONG. Yiddish for snake and a term that has been in London since the C19, though it is more often used in the USA. If you hear an old, sweet melody at dusk, it's Just a Shlong at Twilight.

SHNICKEL, SCHNICKEL. Another Yiddish term, this time for an impotent penis.

SHOOTING IRON, SHOOTING STICK. Both phrases are from the 1860s; the second is American.

SHORT ARM. The military **tool**; a rifle or musket is a long arm; a revolver is a side arm so, of course, the **cock** has to be a short arm.

SHOVE-STRAIGHT. An C18 penis and what the owner planned to do with it.

SILENT FLUTE. The instrument joined the slang orchestra in the 1790s and was played by many until about 1870, since when it has gone into semi-retirement.

SIR MARTIN WAGSTAFF. A knight who was busy during the C16 and C17 but hasn't been heard of much in recent times.

SKYSCRAPER. Derived not from the high building but from the tall masts of sailing ships ruling the waves in the C18 and C19.

SOLLICKER. Slang for an outsized penis heard in the 1940s and 1950s.

SPEAR, SPEAR OF LOVE. More weapons science from the C19, the latter term being favoured by the writers in *The Pearl*. Here is William, the bullish butler, from 'Lady Pockingham', doing what he didn't orter to his boss's daughter: 'Clenching her teeth firmly, and shutting her eyes, she gave another desperate plunge upon William's spear of love and the hymen was broken.'

SPIKE-FAGGOT. Drawn from the C17 word faggot, meaning a woman.

STAND. The manly state reduced to a single word. This was known in the C17 and is still enjoying widespread popularity. Also called a stander and stiff-stander. Here is sex-master Walter in action: 'I closed with her. I had pulled my stiff-stander out. I shook it at her.' God, some fellows are so bloody smooth.

STAR-GAZER. In the C17 and C18 this slang meant an erect penis. Was it a comparison with a telescope or suggesting that the item was waved about in the night air?

STICK AND BANGERS. This is a C19 name for the **cock** and balls.

STIFF AND STOUT. What everyone involved in amorous sport hopes for – a notable erection, described by, wait for it, good old Sir Tommy Urquhart once again.

Star-gazer

STIFF DEITY. The erection as an object of worship – what a charming dream was exposed in this C19 expression.

STING. A nephew of **prick**, a low and common boy born in the C19 and not often heard of these days.

STRETCHER. An C18 way of advertising a substantial **pego** to potential lovers.

STRUNT. This has a good, satisfying sound to it and is a dialect word for the thick part of an animal's tail. The writer Thomas Middleton gave the word a sexual slant in 1608, when he wasn't helping Shakespeare write *Macbeth*.

SUGARSTICK. From the C18 and intended for putting into the **sugar basin**.

SUNDAY MORN. This equals **horn**, which equals an erection. Any questions?

SWORD. Combative imagery from the C17 that is still used today in the term swordsman, an active pussy-chaser and satisfier of desires.

TADGER. Yorkshire dialect, possibly based on tadpole, which drifted south during the C19. Or it may be linked to the term tadge, meaning to join.

TADPOLE BAG. This is slang for the scrotum, home of tadpoles, i.e. semen. Also known as the taddy bag.

TALLYWAG. English dialect, still in use in Derbyshire and Cheshire in the last century; the expression was first noted in the 1790s. A variation occasionally met with is tarriwag. If either word is in the plural, it means the testicles. The forms tallywagger, tallywhacker and tallywocker are found in the USA.

TANNHAUSER. Short-lived, fashionable talk from 1860 when Wagner's dreary opera was decanted on the gullible public in an expanded form featuring the new 'Venusburg' music.

TARSE. An ancient name, whose history goes back to the C11. It fell out of favour round about 1750.

THIRD LEG. Anatomical slang from the 1850s; other legs are the 'best leg of three' and the 'middle leg'.

THRUMSTER. Based on the idea of strumming or thrumming a musical instrument, this word was in tune with public taste from 1680 to 1820.

THUMB OF LOVE. The item with which an C18 male set to work **thumbing** his female.

TICKLE-GIZZARD. A C19 boast, the idea being that the penis is so large that it enters then ascends to the throat.

TICKLE-TAIL. A term from the mid-1600s that was still in use early in the last century; as well as the **tarse**, it could mean a wanton young woman.

TIDDLEY-HOY, TIDDLYPUSH. Two Irish terms from the first half of the C20, both meaning the complete male sexual kit.

TIT-BIT. In the C17 the penis was seen as a tasty morsel waiting to be just gobbled up.

TOOL. With **cock** and **prick** this is one of the Grand Old Men of slang. **Tool** has as an ancestor in the Old Norse *tol* (to make, or to prepare to act) and it was recorded with a sexual meaning in the C16. It is still alive and standing. An American girlfriend of mine had never encountered the term in the USA; soon after learning it in this country she was driving to work and saw a van with the brazen slogan 'East Anglia's Finest Snap-on Tools' painted on the side. She was laughing so hard that she drove the wrong way up a one-way street and met a police car. Which demonstrates that slang can be dangerous.

TOSH. Derived from a dialect word for tusk, this came into the slang lexicon in the C19.

TOOLEYWAG. A name occasionally encountered in the magazines of the 1870s and 1880s: '"Look what your feeling up has done for this, Jenny," said I, shaking my tooleywag at her.'

TRAP-STICK. A name popular from the C16 to the C19 and based on the long, thin stick used in the game trap-ball. NB: trap-sticks (plural) meant the legs and not an extra helping of **trap-stick**.

TRUNCHEON. In North Country dialect, the stomach, but to the pornsmiths of the late C19 another organ entirely, and we're back to that randy sod William the butler in the tale of Lady Pockingham – did the man ever stop fornicating and just buttle? Lucy the maid is sorting him out: '"How is he this morning?" she asked as her hands nervously unbuttoned Mr William's trousers, and grasped his ready truncheon.'

The butler was fortunate, unlike this sad policeman:

> A bobby from Nottingham Junction,
> Whose organ had long ceased to function,

Deceived his good wife
For the rest of her life
With the aid of his constable's truncheon.

Turkey Neck

TURKEY NECK. American 1950s term for the penis
and a slang word the poet Sylvia Plath used in her
1963 novel *The Bell Jar*.

TWANGER. Used for twanging a lady from the C16
to the C20.

TWIDDLE-DIDDLES. The testicles, according to rather
coy slangmongers of the late 1780s.

WAND. What the magician uses to cast his spells. This is from the C19 and a
plain comparison.

WANG, WHANG. This may be an import from the USA in the early C20, though
there is an English dialect verb that means 'to strike',
which may be the true origin. The best literary use is:

Whang

A lady while dining at Crewe
Found an elephant's whang in her stew,
Said the waiter, 'Don't shout
And wave it about
Or the others will all want
one, too.'

WATCH AND SEALS. The
complete set of genitals, in
C19 slang.

WEAPON. Of course it is,
dear; all big and strong, quite right. It
just doesn't look so dangerous when brewer's droop or distiller's dangle has set
in. Not to mention the times when Mr Floppy comes a-calling. A slang term
from the C11, which is still around.

WEDDING TACKLE. Slang from the late C18 and popular still. It refers to the penis and testicles.

WHIBLIN. Up to 1650 or so this was slang for the testicles.

WHIRLIGIGS. A giddy term for the testicles from the C18.

WHISKER-SPLITTER. When this name was thought up circa 1750 it meant a man who was always involved in sexual intrigues and shenanigans, but it rapidly focused on a single male feature.

WHISTLE. The C19 owner of the fleshy instrument may have hoped to get some blasts blown on it at regular intervals.

WHITE OWL. In some rural dialects the barn owl is called the white owl; is there some idea of flying home to roost here?

WHORE-PIPE. A term dating from 1670, made famous by the satirical, randy and rebellious poet Lord Rochester in his lampoon 'Lord Rochester Against his Whore-pipe':

> Was ever Mortal Man like me,
> Continually in Jeopardy,
> And always, silly Prick, by thee!
>
> There's not a Petticoat goes by,
> But from my Cod-piece out you fly,
> Not to be held 'twixt Hand and Thigh.
>
> I never felt a soft, white Hand,
> But Hector-like you strutting stand,
> As if the World you would command.
>
> For all these crying Sins of thine,
> The suffering Part is always mine,
> 'Tis I am crammed with Turpentine.

The thought of using turps to cure the pox is enough to bring tears to the eyes of a statue.

WIFE'S BEST FRIEND. An uncommon venture into matrimony for **John Thomas** but it should be noted that the expression is most often employed in 'shake hands with the wife's best friend', meaning to urinate.

WILLY. He arrives about a hundred years ago and is almost respectable; the term has been used in sex education lessons in secondary schools.

WILTSHIRE. A county famous for scenic views and limp, exhausted members.

WINKLE. Slang generally used by small children and those at school; it was first heard in the 1860s.

WINKY. A small and feeble organ was called this in the 1870s. It was sometimes spelled winkie but that failed to improve matters.

WOOD. A word for the penis from the early C19; in recent years it has reappeared but now meaning an erection. (See **woodsman** in Chapter 7 for more information.)

WOODEN SPOON. The **stiff deity** in a 1920s setting.

WORM. Given the ultra-flexible, ever-bending physique of the worm, this is probably not a compliment.

WRIGGLING POLE. Invented in the late C17 by the writer D'Urfey and never a widely used expression.

YARD. A venerable word, one of the earliest slang names but no longer in fashion. **Yard** has been traced back to the Old Teutonic *gardja*, meaning a pole, and the Latin *hasta*, meaning a spear.

YUM-YUM. From the C19, an expression of delight that also meant the penis and vagina.

4. ROUNDED GLORIES

The breasts and buttocks are counted as secondary sexual characteristics and have attracted fewer names than the vagina and penis, though in the latter part of the twentieth century breasts received increasing interest and acquired more and more nicknames. (Female breasts, that is; I found only one term for the male **dugs** – and that was from trade slang.)

Our Bard Who Chickens Out has a line or five of verse on breasts:

> A woman has bosoms, a bust or a breast,
> Those lily-white swellings that bulge 'neath her vest.
> They are towers of ivory, sheaves of new wheat;
> In a moment of passion, ripe apples to eat.
> You may speak of her nipples as small rings of fire
> With hardly a question of raising her ire,
> But by Rabelais' beard will she throw fits
> If you speak of them roundly as good honest —.

Attitudes have changed since the 1940s; throwing fits at the mention of her **tits** is not a standard reaction today. Yelling, 'Sexist shit!' while kneeing your **nuts** is more likely.

As with other areas of sexual slang, the oldest terms are once-respectable words that have slithered down the linguistic social ladder and wound up in the dirt. **Tit** in the sixteenth century was a shortening of **teat** (nipple) and was also used to describe a young girl, a prostitute and the vagina at different times in the eighteenth and nineteenth centuries. The word was applied to a small horse and I heard it used in that sense at sales in the 1960s. The shift to **tit/titties** meaning breasts began about 1740, but the term became general only during the 1800s.

Arse is another example of a changed status. This fine old word has ancestors in most North European languages, like Old Norse, Old High German and

Friesian, and living cousins in the Icelandic *ars* and Dutch *aars*. Its origins lie far back in time and to the east; **arse** is descended from the Greek *oros*. By AD1000 the word was at home in Anglo-Saxon; birdwatchers who note the arrival and departure of the charming (and once widely eaten) wheatear may not know that the name is a modern version of white-arse, the bird's old name. And the penguin was once called the arse-foot.

Until 1660 or so **arse** went cheerfully through the world, minding its own business. Then the Language Bleachers moved in; **arse** was declared impolite, unfit for society and banished to the lower depths. For several centuries it lived in a linguistic leper colony, but it has been edging up the ladder again, from the slang rung to the colloquial one. When modified to **ass** (a game Shakespeare liked to play) the word is held to be less offensive. (NB **arse** is used for the anus and the buttocks; nicknames for both features appear in this list.)

Try out a few of the following to amuse and bewilder your friends and loved ones.

ABAFT THE WHEELHOUSE. Picturesque US Navy slang for the **ass** during the period 1900–1920.

AFFIES, AFFEYS. Dialect term for the female breasts. This may have started life as a local accent rendering of **apples**.

AMPERSAND, &. Reading primers in the C19 frequently printed the ampersand after the letters of the alphabet and some slangster made use of the fact to describe the **bum**.

ANTIPODES. The bottom of the Earth indicated by slang popular from 1850 until the early part of the C20.

APPLES. One of many fruit images for breasts, this one dating from the C18. The word is also used for the testicles. It served as part of an elaboration in the 1790s: the apple dumpling shop. That's a phrase I find it difficult to imagine somebody murmuring in a lover's ear.

Apples

ARRIS. An example of the complex nature of rhyming slang. **Arris** is short for Aristotle, rhyming with bottle, which is a reduction of **bottle and glass – arse**.

ARS MUSICA. Latin for 'musical art' and refers to the wide range of symphonic and orchestral effects the anus is capable of producing. In the C18 this was a great joke.

ARSE. Part of the English language from about AD1000 and socially acceptable until the 1660s. Now edging back into acceptance in phrases like 'arse over tip' and 'not know your arse from your elbow'.

ASHCAN. A name for the backside used in America from 1900 to about 1910.

ASS. At first glance the all-American arsehole, but Shakespeare was there first (see Chapter 7) and **ass**, though standard American usage, was only recorded in the C19.

> Rosalinda, a pretty young lass,
> Had a truly magnificent ass;
> Not rounded and pink
> As you probably think –
> It was grey, had long ears and ate grass.

AVOCADOS. An American word for the bust used in the 1930s. The avocado pear reached Great Britain in the C17 and was called 'midshipman's butter' because the Royal Navy fed the fruit to its crews. The avocado did not become a popular food in this country until the 1960s and the slang for breasts never caught on here.

BABY'S PUBLIC HOUSE. A boozer's view of the breasts recorded in 1884.

BACK DOOR. The anus in C18 slang; the expression is still used.

BACK LAND. A description of the bottom imported from the Caribbean during the C18.

BACKSLICE. Round about 1850 slangsters adopted this word for the anus.

BAGS. Slangsters of the 1930s decided this word was an acceptable way of naming the breasts.

BALCONY. Substantial and cantilevered breasts, jutting out far enough to stand a candelabra on; the word was used regularly in the 1940s. A 'balcony' bra can still be bought today.

BALLYNOCACK. From Ireland and from the C18 this word for the anus literally means 'shit town'.

BARGE-ARSE. Nothing to do with shipping, but a C19 comment on the size of somebody's southern aspect.

BATI, BATTI, BATTY. West Indian slang for the buttocks, first heard circa 1910 then forgotten by the general public until its revival in the 1980s.

BEAUTIFUL PAIR OF BROWN EYES. Mid-C20 slang for the breasts, punning on the colour of some nipples and areolas.

BEHIND. Noted first in the 1780s, **behind** is really a semi-genteel euphemism more than slang. It is still in regular use.

BERKELEYS. This is not a collection of **Berkeley hunts,** but the bosom in slang based on the Romany word *berk,* meaning breast.

BIM. This sounds like a coy **bum** and enjoyed a limited popularity in the 1930s.

BLIND CHEEKS. The rump in slang, first noted in 1690. The saying then was 'kiss my blind cheeks', which is a little subtler than 'kiss my arse'.

BLIND CUPID. The bottom, according to slangmongers of the late C18.

BLIND EYE. A name for the anus thought up about 1750.

BLOT. An Australian rectum of the 1940s.

BLUBBER, BLUBBERBAGS. Perhaps dragged ashore from a whaler, these words for the breasts appeared in the C18; **blubberbags** lasted into the C20.

BOOBIES. An American term for **Bristols** invented in the 1930s, but clearly related to much older terms like **bubbies**.

BOTTIE, BOTTY. Genteelisms for the rear issuing from the demure section of C19 society and still heard today.

BOTTLE AND GLASS. (See **Arris**.)

BOUNCERS. About 1840 this indicated large breasts; the word went missing after a few years only to reappear in the 1950s.

Bubs

BRISTOLS, BRISTOL CITIES, BRISTOL BITS. Popular rhyming slang for **titties** all dating from the late C19 and early C20.

BUBS, BUBBIES. Before **tits** became the standard word, breasts were **bubs** and **bubbies**. Dr Johnson once confessed that the sight of actresses' bubs on display 'made my penis quiver'.

BUFFERS. Late C19 slang for breasts.

BUM. The buttocks, from an old word (dating back to 1387) that has gone downmarket over the centuries, though Shakespeare, Ben Jonson and Dean Swift all found it good enough to use. **Bum** is not a reduction of 'bottom' as some believe but a word based on the sound of a rump landing on a flat surface, like a bench or chair. Only in the 1790s did the word 'lose caste', in Partridge's words. By 1840 it was completely in disgrace. But it has survived.

Variations include bumbo, bum-bum, bumkin and bumbazine.

BUMPS, BUMPERS. Large breasts in mid-C20 slang.

BUNGHOLE. The anus in the C16; the word was revived during the first half of the C20.

BUSHEL BUBBY. In the 1780s this was the way a woman with large breasts was described. A bushel was a dry measure of eight gallons of grain or fruit; it is no longer in use.

CABMAN'S RESTS. Rhyming slang for the breasts from the London of the 1880s.

CAMERA OBSCURA. Latin meaning dark room and designating the anus, again in the 1880s.

CAN. A late-C19 description of the backside, but now usually a name for the lavatory (especially in the USA).

CHARLEYS, CHARLIES. This slang for **bubs** arrived in 1840 and is still heard today. Nobody knows where it arrived from, though a Romany word *charo* (to meddle with or touch) has been suggested, along with the substantial **Bristols** of Charles II's various mistresses. If that is the case, the expression was a bloody long time arriving because Charles II died in 1685.

CHARLIE WHEELERS. Australian for **bubs** from the middle of the C20; the name is that of a painter celebrated for his nude studies.

CHARMS. The C19 showing a softer side in this slang for the bust, dating from circa 1855.

CHEEKS. The buttocks were first described this way in 1750; the term has persisted and is quite acceptable.

COCONUTS. Large breasts were called by this name at the end of the C19 and in the early C20.

CORYBUNGO. A fine, well-sprung word for the bottom that was first used by professional boxers circa 1850 to 1900. Its origins are obscure.

CREAM JUGS, CREAMERS. At the beginning of the C20 these names for the breasts were used in Australia.

CRUPPER. Technically the term for a horse's rump, but it has been applied to the human stern – usually in a humorous way – since the C16.

CUPID'S KETTLEDRUMS. You can't beat the C18 for poetic conceits. This image of the breasts appeared about 1740.

DAIRIES. The maternal, nourishing breasts in this C18 term. Partridge in his dictionary gives 'air the dairies' and 'sport the dairies' as slang for flashing the bust.

DAIRY ARRANGEMENTS. The phrase was popular from 1910 until the end of the 1920s.

DATE. New Zealand and Australian slang for the anus, first recorded about 1910.

DEADEYE. A late-C19 and early-C20 term for the anus.

DECK CARGO. A nautical description of large **charleys**.

DIDDIES, DIDDYS. A variation of **titties** that appeared in the anonymous *The Quaker's Opera* in the 1780s.

DOLLIES. Irish breasts in the 1950s and 1960s.

DOPEY. The bottom in the C18, but before that it was a way of naming a beggar's ladylove.

DOT. The rectum circa 1950. The slang was fashionable in New Zealand and Australia.

DOUBLE JUG. The **bum** from the C17 to the C19, presumably in large helpings.

DRODDUM. The rump in this 1860 coinage.

DUDS. A mid-C20 New Zealand name for the breasts.

DUFF. The **arse** in the 1890s.

DUGS. Breasts or nipples, according to Partridge, who says that since the 1880s this vulgarism can be Standard English 'if used as a strong pejorative'. So saying, 'Darling, your dugs are lovely' is slang but 'Your dugs are bloody 'orrible!' is Standard English. You live and you learn.

DUMMOCK. The behind circa 1850, described by a word that may be composed of the Romany *dumo* (back) and the '-ock' from buttocks.

DUMPLINGS. This slang usually refers to particularly large and round breasts and has been cooking since 1700.

umplings

DUTCH DUMPLINGS. The buttocks, according to early-C20 slang.

EYE OF THE ARSE. A way of seeing where you've been, described in Irish slang created in around 1905.

FEAK. In the early C19 this word was used to name the buttocks. Its origin is obscure.

FEEDING BOTTLES. The breasts in the view of slangsters circa 1900–10.

FERN. The buttocks, according to Americans in the 1950s.

FLIP-FLOPS. Oz-speak for the breasts in the 1920s.

FOREBUTTOCKS. The breasts described in the 1720s by the poet Alexander Pope. Pope was a small man, a mere five feet tall. A young nobleman and the author Colley Cibber (an enemy of Pope) wanted to discover if the poet (tiny but perfect in every detail) was virile; they invited Pope to tea and made sure it was served by:

> … a damsel with charms sufficient to tempt the little-tiny
> manhood of Mr Pope into the next room with her … I threw open
> the door and found this little hero, like a terrible Tom-Tit, pertly
> perching upon the mount of love! I laid hold of his heels, and drew
> him down safe from his danger.

Poor little Pope. With an enemy like Cibber, who needs enemies? But Pope's poetry has lasted and is read and studied today, while Cibber's is not. Pope offered Cibber this advice – perhaps in revenge for the interrupted coition:

> Cibber! Write all thy Verses upon Glasses,
> The only way to save 'em from our Arses.

FRECKLE. A 1960s name for the rectum.

FUGO. A designation for the anus used in the C17 and C18 and based on an old word for a fart.

FUN. The rump or fundament in slang popular from 1680–1750.

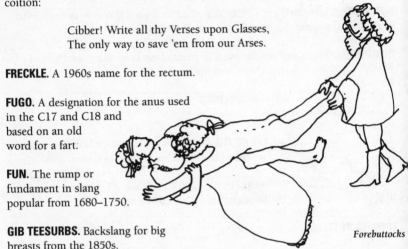

Forebuttocks

GIB TEESURBS. Backslang for big breasts from the 1850s.

GLOBES. The 1860s way of saying **bubbies**. The word has a rather literary and somewhat genteel sound. Our pornographic pals at *The Pearl* found the description useful in 1870: '... unable to restrain his excitability, he spent all over her lovely mossy mount and belly, some of the sperm going quite up to the alabaster globes which adorned her heaving chest.'

Shakespeare used **globe** for the breasts in his plays.

GOAT. The rear end of a human being was given this name in 1848, but shrugged it off very quickly. The goat was probably happy about that, too.

GOOSEBERRY GRINDER. In the C19 this slang for the posterior was generally heard in the expression 'Ask Bogey the gooseberry grinder', the age's version of 'Ask my arse!'

GUNGA. The rectum, according to this word from 1940s New Zealand.

HAND WARMERS. Slang for the breasts created in Australia in the early C20.

HANGERS. The **globes** in the view of Australian and American slang circa 1930.

HEAVERS. This could be based on the celebrated heaving bosom of literature; the slang first appeared in the C17 and lasted for two centuries.

HEINIE. The **arse** in a First World War creation based on the German name Heinrich.

HUFF. To slangsters of the 1880s this indicated the buttocks.

JACKSIE, JAXSIE. The behind, as spoken of by the Royal Navy and the Army from the 1870s onwards. The word is based on a 1850s term for the buttocks, jacksy-pardy.

JUBILEE. Popular in low and sporting circles, this slang for the rear was minted in 1887 for Queen Victoria's Golden Jubilee, coming, as it did, at the arse-end of the century.

JUFF. A rare term for the buttocks.

JUTLAND. The posterior, especially substantial, projecting ones. In the 1960s snug-fitting trousers were called arse-jutters. Is the expression still in use?

KEEL. Buttocks from Scotland from the late C19 to the mid-C20.

KEESTER, KEISTER. Invented in the USA in the mid-C19, this initially meant the back pocket of trousers. By obvious extension it covered the whole **ass**.

KHYBER PASS. Rhyming slang for the latter end and dating from the 1890s, the First World War or the 1940s, depending on which book you look it up in.

KNOBBIES. Slang for the **heavers** that arrived and departed in the first half of the last century.

KNOCKERS. A word for the breasts first used in the 1930s and still working hard for its living.

LOTTIES. Slang for the breasts in use circa 1890–1910 and based on the formidable frontage of the music-hall star Lottie Collins.

LUNGS. American **bubs** during the 1950s.

MANCHESTER CITIES, MANCHESTERS. Simple rhymes please simple minds. A northern version of **Bristols**. In the USA Jersey City provides the rhyme.

MEAT MARKET. An edible and commercial image from the C19 – this means the breasts.

MEDLAR. An image of the anus based on the shape of the pear-like fruit and thought up in the C17.

Milkshop

MILKSHOP, MILKWALK. The nursing, practical view of breasts from about 1850 and, in the case of **milkshop** still used by some folk in Islington, where I heard it in 2000. In the 1950s the word milk-bar was favoured, after the hang-out of teenage tearaways, Teddy boys and other menaces to society. In 1930s Australia 'milk bottle' was a favoured name.

MONOCULAR EYEGLASS. A galumphing piece of 1860 joshing that describes the anus. Laugh? I thought I'd never start.

MOON. One of the C18 terms for the bottom; later on it became a verb for displaying the rear end, performed by people who keep their brains in the part being displayed.

MOUNTAINS. Very large breasts in mid-C20 slang.

NANCY. From 1810–1910 this word was used in the saying 'Ask my nancy' (ask my arse). It does not seem to have had any homosexual connotations.

NATURE'S FOUNTS. A very elegant means of indicating the **knockers** during the early C19.

NAY-NAYS. What made somebody in the 1950s conjure up this way of speaking about the female **forebuttocks**? Sometimes slang is most peculiar.

NETHERLANDS. Slang from the C18 more often used to describe the genitals but sometimes applied to the **arse**.

NOCK. This C18 word means the anus, when not doing duty for the vagina or copulation.

NOCKANDRO. The anus in 1611 described by a word that is probably compounded of 'notch' and the Greek *andros*, meaning man. Literary showing off rather than slang, I feel.

NORKS. The breasts in 1950s Australia, named for the buttermaker Norco Ltd of New South Wales.

NUBBIES. Aussie-talk for **dumplings** from about 1890.

PANTERS. Slang for the breasts that was used from 1880–1900. The expression was based on the older panter (heart). Which was a play on 'the hart panteth after water' in Psalm 42.

PAP-FEEDER, PAPS. The breasts are seen as the source of nourishment in these C19 terms.

PART THAT GOES OVER THE FENCE LAST. This is a fine example of homespun, rural American long-windedness meaning the **arse**.

PATOOTIE. The **bum** in American 1920s slang; the word shifted meaning and became a general endearment before spreading to the UK, Australia and New Zealand. It is sometimes shortened to patoot.

PEARLY KING. Rhyming slang for **ring**, a Cockney slangmonger's effort.

PIPE AND DRUM. Bum in early-C20 rhyming slang.

PLASTER OF PARIS. The posterior in rhyming slang. (See **Arris**.)

PLUMS. Breasts that are especially shapely and pleasing. The slang may go back to the late C17. The word can also refer to the vagina.

POONTS. A full, heavy-sounding word you can almost squeeze, indicating the breasts; it was popular from 1850–1870.

PORTHOLE. A basic image for the anus, first employed in that sense about 1660. It sometimes referred to the vagina.

PRAT. A name for the buttocks used by Harman in 1567 and still employed in pratfall.

PRIZE FAGGOTS. The breasts in slang dating from 1890. NB: the faggots here have nothing to do with sexual orientation but are a kind of meatball made of pork, breadcrumbs and herbs. Faggot is also a slang word for a woman.

PROMINENT BITS. Tailors' rhyming slang for the male breasts, useful guides when measuring a client for a waistcoat. The term dates from the early C20.

QUOIT. Australian for the anus in the 1930s and 1940s.

RACKS OF MEAT. This C19 description of the bosom was often shortened to racks.

RING. The anus from about 1870 onwards. Also a whole cycle of long-winded operas by Wagner.

ROBY DOUGLAS. A sample of Royal Navy talk from 1780 in a description of the anus, using the name of a sad case with 'one eye and a stinking breath'. Not a shipmate a sailor would want to sling his hammock alongside.

ROUNDEYE. The all-seeing anus in the C19.

ROUND MOUTH. A rather twee name for the **ring**, first noted in 1810. Even more arch is the extension: Brother Roundmouth. Can you guess what it means when the good brother speaks? Of course you can.

SATCHEL-ARSE. A large rump covered by baggy or ill-cut trousers, according to speakers in 1823. A 'satchel-arsed fellow' or 'satchel-arsed son of a whore' was not a welcome companion.

SEAT OF HONOUR, SEAT OF SHAME, SEAT OF VENGEANCE. Three phrases from the C19 conveying different ideas about the buttocks.

SITTING-ROOM. The coy side of the C19, all antimacassars and aspidistras, describing the **arse**.

SPICE ISLAND. A name for the fundament, stressing its ripe and fruity odours. The first voyage to the exotic isle was recorded in 1810.

STERN. This is more of a euphemism than slang and provided a polite, rather jaunty use from the C19.

SUNDAY FACE. This is C19 slang for the buttocks. No, I don't know why, either.

Satchel-arse

SWINGERS. From 1919–29 Australian **plums** received this slang name.

TAIL. This word for the buttocks has suffered much the same fate as **arse**; it was Standard English from the C14 until 1750, when it was declared unsavoury. Taking offence, **tail** moved to North America and has done very well there. **Tail** can also mean copulation, the penis and the female sex organs.

> On her bosom a beauteous young frail
> Had illumined the price of her tail;

> And on her behind,
> For the sake of the blind,
> The same is embroidered in Braille.

TALE OF TWO CITIES. The bubs in the rhyming slang of 1950–9.

TAN TRACK. Not a dirt road, but C19 slang for the fundament.

TEATS. Not really slang, but one of those technical terms that nobody ever seems really comfortable using.

TEWEL. Chaucer's word for the anus as a means of excretion, literally meaning pipe. The word is sometimes spelled tuel.

THOUSAND PITIES. Late-C19 rhyming slang for titties.

THREEPENNY BITS. Rhyming slang indicating the forebuttocks in the late C19. It also occurs as thrups, broken down from thrupenny bits.

TITS, TITTIES. As mentioned at the start of this chapter, these words established themselves during the C19 and replaced older terms like bubbies.

> To his bride said the lynx-eyed detective,
> 'Can it be that my eyesight's defective?
> Has your east tit the least bit
> The best of the west tit,
> Or is it a trick of perspective?'

TOBY. A word for the buttocks recorded in 1675. It often appeared in the phrase 'tickle his toby', meaning a thrashing.

TOCHIS, TOKHES, TUCHIS. The Yiddish word for posterior, often reduced to tush or toosh. It has been used in English since the late C19.

TOORALOORALS. An 1880s manner of naming the bosom.

TOP BOLLOCKS. The breasts as described in late-C19 military slang.

TOP BUTTOCKS. Again the breasts, again from the late C19, but without the military influence this time.

TOWNS AND CITIES. The **tooraloorals** in the rhyming slang of the late C19.

TWATTLING STRINGS. In the early C17 John Florio either recorded or invented the word twattle, meaning a fart; the **twattling strings** are the anal sphincter as a sound controller. The expression has not been in common (or any other) use since the C18.

TWO FAT CHEEKS AND NE'ER A NOSE. A long-winded phrase for the **arse** from the C19.

UDDERS. A slang word for very large breasts.

UPPER WORKS. A description of the female breasts in 1870. In Australia and New Zealand the preferred term was 'upper deck', which became popular during the 1930s.

VAN NECK, MISS/MRS. A name slangmongers slapped on women with big busts from 1770 to about 1810.

WATERMELONS. A 1950s and 1960s description of large or very large breasts.

WESTPHALIA. In the 1890s hams from Westphalia were considered a delicacy and the name was transferred to the buttocks.

WHERE THE MONKEY SHOVES HIS NUTS. A catch phrase from the 1890s. The nuts are shoved 'where the sun don't shine' or right up the anus.

WINDMILL. The anus described by the slang of 1811. Women were said to have no fortunes but their mills, wind and water, both of which could be sold. (See Chapter 2 for **water-mill**.)

Where The Monkey Shoves His Nuts

WINDSOR CASTLE. A palatial rhyme for arsehole dating back to the 1880s. In the boastful ballad 'The Finest Fucking Family in the Land' the singer's father 'sells his arsehole to the Guards at Windsor Castle', which is coals to Newcastle.

WINDWARD PASSAGE. A piece of C18 slang for the **blind eye** that was obsolete by 1810.

5. NAMES FOR THE GAMES

Sex is a kind of intuitive art in itself, an art made largely by the human body on levels our frontal cortex can only partly imagine.
Sallie Tisdale: *Talk Dirty to Me*

Considerable amounts of creative power have been used to find names for sexual acts and their pleasurable sensations. This list of mainly heterosexual behaviours offers a sample of the slang thought up over the centuries. The styles range from the comical to the brutal, with origins are varied as falconry and gardening.

The anonymous 1940s bard quoted in Chapter 2 has the following advice on the polite way to request coition:

> Though a lady repel your advance, she'll be kind
> Just as long as you 'intimate' what's on your mind.
> You can tell her you're hungry, you need to be swung,
> You may ask her to see how your etchings are hung.
> You may mention the ashes that need to be hauled;
> Put the lid on her sauce-pan ('lay' isn't too bald);
> But the moment you're forthright, get ready to duck:
> The girl isn't born yet who'll stand for 'Let's —'.

Times have changed, have they not? This sad poet would be horrified to learn that his ever-so-naughty word is no longer a major shock to human systems.

In fact, **fuck** is one of the words that have moved from Standard English into slang. Its exact history has yet to be unravelled; Eric Partridge believed it could be traced back to the Latin *pungare* (to strike), which is more likely than some histories offered. Ultimately **fuck** may go back to the ancient Sanskrit word for a bull: *ukshan*.

In 1503 the Scottish poet William Dunbar used **fuck** and nobody commented. It was included in an early dictionary, *Worlde of Wordes*, in 1598, along with two much older words, **sard** and **swive**. But a century later **fuck** was considered unsavoury, and soon after it became one of the Great Unspoken, its offensiveness – to some people – equalled only by **cunt**. Writers who used either term were persecuted, prosecuted and despised.

Now it would be hard to get through a day near other people without hearing one or other word used as abuse, their intimate and tender aspects eroded by overwork.

The slang covered here includes old favourites as well as the forgotten, neglected and recondite. Be kind to some obscure term and give it an outing; whisper it tenderly to your partner – along with an explanation of what you're saying.

ABOUT HER. Intercourse in C18 terms, usually in the phrase 'to have about her'.

ADAMISE. A biblical, Edenic verb created in the C19.

ARMOUR, FIGHTING IN. In the C18 this meant using a condom. They were made of sheep gut and considered very reliable. The best were sold by Mrs Philips, whose shop sign was THE GOLDEN FAN AND RISING SUN. In her 1776 advert she wrote:

> To guard yourself from shame or fear,
> Votaries to Venus, hasten here;
> None in my wares e'er found a flaw,
> Self preservation's nature's law.

For many years the usual name for a condom was Mrs Philips' purse.

Armour

ARSELINGS COUP, GET AN. A woman's perspective of intercourse: arselings equating to backwards and coup meaning a blow. Being knocked over and thumped does not suggest much tender, loving care.

ASS, HAVE A PIECE OF. A slice of American slang from the late C19 and early C20, with **ass** being the American for **arse**. At least, I hope that is the meaning. If not, the people at the Hampstead Donkey Refuge will hear of this outrage, you pervert.

BACKGAMMON. To sodomise, the act being performed by a 'backgammon player', of course. The term was used for about a century from 1740.

BACK-SCUTTLE. To enter a woman from behind, in C19 slang; it also means sodomy.

BAGPIPE. A term for fellatio in the C18 and the C19. In recent years it has been used for intercourse with a partner's armpit.

BALLUM RANCUM. An C18 dance at which all partners were naked and all the women were for hire.

BASKET-MAKING. This slang was widely used from the 1750s to the early C19. A pregnant woman had 'a kid in the basket'.

BED, TO. More like plain speaking than slang, and with us since the C16.

BEEF, BE IN HER. Intercourse according to slang coined in the late C18, and on everyone's lips until the 1850s. The female participant was said to 'take in beef'. Different versions that were less popular are 'do some beef' and 'have a bit of beef'.

Bagpipe

BELLY BUMPER. The usual phrase was 'get a belly bumper', meaning a pregnancy after two bellies had bumped together without taking proper precautions. A 1703 dance tune was called 'The Maiden's Blush, or Bump in her Belly'.

BIT. A very male view of sex from the 1850s, reducing the entire process to **do a bit** or 'have a bit' or 'get a bit'.

BIT OF HARD FOR A BIT OF SOFT. London low talk of the 1840s to 1860s – graphic enough but not very original.

BIT OF SNUG, HAVE A. Most often used in the C19 for sexual intercourse, but sometimes indicating the penis.

BLANKET HORNPIPE. One of the dance-inspired images and sounding distinctly nautical; did jolly jack tars brag of their nifty footwork performing this in 1810, when the expression appeared? Nelson and Emma Hamilton must have performed it often. The slang is based on a term that was already two hundred years old: 'blanket-love' was extramarital sex.

BLINDFOLD BIT. A peculiar piece of slang from the C19; does it imply that the vagina is an eye blinded by the labia folded over it?

BLOCK. An early-C20 expression that has disappeared.

BLOW JOB. Fellatio from the US of the 1940s.

BLOW THE GROUNDSELS. During the C17 lovers **blowing the groundsels** were shagging on the floor.

BLOW THROUGH HER. An exclusively male expression from the 1890s, no longer encountered.

BLOW YOUR BULKHEADS. An extremely satisfying orgasm. The phrase probably has a naval origin.

BOARD HER. Sounds nautical and piratical, but this seems to have been used mainly in porn of the C19.

BOB. Drawn from a country word meaning 'to hit' in the C19.

BOFF. A verb from the late C19 and early C20, which reappeared in the 1970s, it is claimed. The use was always upper-crust rather than street slang

BOMBAY ROLL. Intercourse between the breasts, with the discharge forming a 'pearl necklace'.

BONE. An informant tells me this was military slang in the 1880s but I have not been able to trace it. Presumably it links with boner as an erection, or the Latin for good, *bona*.

BOTTOM-FUCKING. A peculiarly genteel expression that appears in C19 porn and seldom in real life, one suspects. This was Lady Pockingham's introduction to the word and deed:

> He showed me a series of splendid drawings illustrating the way to enjoy bottom-fucking. He could see I was tremendously excited … anointing my tight little bum-hole with some ointment and putting some also on the shaft of his prick, he made me push my bottom out behind but 'Ah! Ah! No, no, I can't bear it!' I exclaimed …

BOUNCE. Like many other words featuring violent (or potentially violent) action, this was introduced by slangmongers towards the end of the C19. It was still in use in London in the 1970s.

BREAD AND BUTTER FASHION. In 1742 an amusement park called Ranelagh Gardens opened in Chelsea, offering food, drink, music and (unofficially) sex. The place was soon nicknamed the Bread and Butter Warehouse and the chief activity there became the **bread and butter fashion**.

BREAK A LANCE WITH HER. Based on the tournaments of the Middle Ages and the spear still used by lancer regiments in the C19.

BRIM. An animal metaphor – brimming is the technical term for mating a sow and boar. The slang was used from 1600–1750.

BRING ON. Foreplay C16 style and not to be confused with **bring off**, which means to achieve orgasm. 'Bring on the china' was an elaboration used in the first part of the C20.

BRONK. Country dialect from the 1830s for interfemoral intercourse. (Before you reach for the dictionary, interfemoral means 'between the thighs'.) More recently the word has been used to describe an erection.

BROWN, BIT OF. Slang for anal intercourse first used in the C19 and still current.

BRUSH. Generally found in the phrase 'have a brush with'; when applied to a woman it means sex and when applied to a man it means a fight. The slang has been in use since the 1750s.

BUCK, GO TO. The buck here is a man as a male animal and the term is used of a woman eager for sex. Or, to quote the *New Canting Dictionary* (1725), 'a wanton Woman, who is desirous of Male Conversation'.

BUGGER. Is this slang, swearing, a technical description of anal intercourse (generally between men) in Standard English, or what? The word was recorded in 1555 and is an Anglicisation of the French *bougre*, imported in 1340. The word *bougre* may derive from *Bulgarus*, Bulgarians having been condemned as heretics. In some American states the term also covers intercourse with animals; this undergraduate would have felt home there:

Bugger

There was a young student
of John's
Who wanted to bugger
the swans,
But a loyal hall porter
Said, 'Sir, take my daughter,
Them birds are reserved
for the dons.'

BULL. A verb used circa 1710–1810 and giving rise to the proverb 'He who bulls the cow must keep the calf.'

BUM. The full slang expression (from the C19) is 'have a bit of bum'. It is not sodomy but vaginal intercourse and done by someone who sees a woman as simply a **bum shop** (a vagina).

BUMBASTE. Back in the C16 and C17 this meant a beating on the buttocks. In the C18 it took on the sexual meaning.

BUMBLE. The poet John Dryden used this in his work *The Kind Keeper*, 1680. It carries overtones of fumbling and inexperience or semi-impotence.

BUMFIDDLE. Not sodomy but copulation is indicated by this C19 word.

BURNING SHAME. An C18 cabaret turn that involved a horizontal woman becoming a candlestick, with the candle inserted in her vagina.

BUSHY PARK, TAKE A STROLL IN. (See Chapter 2 for details of **Bushy Park**.) This is the 1860s version of the sport; in 1810 it was 'be at Bushy Park'.

BUSINESS. Professional slang used by the C17 and C18 jilts, wagtails, mawkes, trugmoldies, Mother Midnights, Fleet Street doves, bunters, Pickethatch vestals, punchable nuns, blowzabellas, fireships, St John's Wood donas, or plain whores. For those ladies 'to do the business' meant **mowing** for money. The slang is still heard today.

BUSTLE PUNCHING. A C19 term for frottage, i.e. obtaining sexual pleasure by rubbing against another person. These days it is difficult to avoid the rubbing in a rush-hour Tube train, but the pleasure is not always shared.

BUTTERED BUN. Lying with a **buttered bun** was the C17 version of sloppy seconds. Grose's *Dictionary* has this comment in 1785: 'One lying with a woman that has just lain with another man, is said to have a buttered bun.' Earlier on the words were used for a mistress.

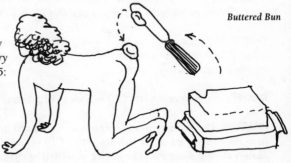

Buttered Bun

BUTTFUCK. An American way of saying **bottom-fucking** in the 1960s. An American friend of mine described an unpleasant man as 'a guy who'd buttfuck Bambi'.

BUTTOCK BALL, DANCE AT. In the 1790s it meant coition, with both the buttocks and balls being involved in the proceedings. A **buttock ball** was a dance at which the only women invited were whores.

BUTTON LURK. An Australian term from the early C20 meaning unprotected sex.

BUTTONHOLE. A multi-role word that could mean fucking, the female sex organ and female masturbation. All uses seem to date from about 1870.

CATERWAUL. The yowling of randy cats, when the tom mounts the queen, became in the C16 human foreplay.

CATSO, POT THE. No, not an obscure piece of advice to a snooker or pool player, but C17 slang for nookie. **Catso** could also mean either a rogue or the balls. Take your pick.

CAULIFLOWER. The usual expression was 'have a bit of cauliflower'; the slang was first used in the C18 and then reappeared in the 1990s. (See **cauliflower** in Chapter 2.)

CAULK. A choice of meanings for this one; it may refer to a male bird mating with a female or plugging the planks of a ship's hull to make it watertight.

CAVAULTING. Intercourse in the language of the late C17 to early C19. The image is from a horse cavorting and the word was extracted from the Low Latin for horse, *caballus*.

CHAFER. In use from the late C19 to about 1910, this is related to **chauver**.

CHARVER. The Romany words for coition, to rub and meddling with somebody have been suggested as the parents of this C19 verb. It mutated to charva in Parlary theatre slang and, like **chafer**, is related to **chauver**.

CHAUVER. A word for intercourse that arrived in 1840; as well as being related to northern dialect chauve, meaning to warm up, **chauver** has links with the French *chauffer* (to heat). Chauvering donnas and chauvering molls were dimber morts (lovely ladies) not averse to hawking their mutton, if the price was right.

CHAWS. Another term that can claim cousinship to **chauver** and in use from 1860–1900.

CHIVALRY. Sadly, this does not date back to days of yore, when maidens were fair, knights were bold, men were men and sheep were scared fleeceless, but only to 1780 or so. In the following century slangsters warped it to chivarley.

CHUCK A TREAD. When I first saw this 1860 phrase for **fucking** I thought it was linked to 'tread', the mating of fowl, or was perhaps an old version of throwing a fuck into somebody. It turns out to be linked to a word for a prostitute used from 1630–1890, 'treadle', as in a foot-operated lever of the same name.

CLICKET. A sporting and rural word, well known to huntsmen and naturalists. Mating foxes are said 'to be at clicket' in Standard English; the application to humans commenced in the 1600s and had passed its speak-by date in the late C18.

CLITORISE. A slide-rule, computer-simulation sort of slang for an intimate and enjoyable activity.

COCK, GIVE COCK, TAKE COCK. A simple verb, whose slight extensions came into slang in the late C18 and gained strength during the next two hundred years. In the 1980s a girlfriend and I were touring the Cotswolds; she went into a pub loo and, after fifteen minutes, had failed to emerge. I began to worry. The landlady said, 'Oh, she'll be reading the questionnaire.' The previous summer an unknown loo-user had inscribed 108 questions headed 'Giving cock, taking cock: the facts' on a cubicle's walls. Apparently very few women could resist reading the whole opus and the bar staff were used to seeing irritated men hanging about.

COCK INN, STAY AT. Very obvious phrase first used about 1730 and still employed today.

COCK LOFT, PLAY A GAME IN. From 1650–1750 this was a popular way of referring to fornication.

COME, COME OFF. The most widely used description of orgasm from the century before last to the present day. Is it still slang or simply a popular term that is not yet polite?

COME ABOUT ME. Said of a man by a woman if she elected to use slang about 1850. It has a seafaring flavour, like 'come aloft', which has the double task of meaning an erection as well as a fuck.

COVER. Technical language from the stud farm; a stallion is said to cover a mare. Sir Thomas Urquhart may have been the first to apply the word to humans when he did so in 1653.

CRACK A JUDY, CRACK A JUDY'S TEACUP. To deflower a virgin, according to C19 speech; Judy was the name used for Everywoman, like Tom, Dick or Harry for Everyman.

CREAM, TAKE IN. A feminine view of intercourse in the late 1890s.

CUDDLE MY CUDDIE. An obscure phrase from the mid-C19; in some dialects cuddie or cuddy is the name for a donkey.

CULLY-SHANGY. Culls are the balls but nobody knows what shangy is/was. That did not bother the C19 slang-mongers who coupled the words.

Cuddy

DANCE THE REEL O' STUMPIE. A Scottish expression for a universal sport in the C18. And the answer to the Sassenach FAQ 'What's worn under the kilt?' is: 'Nothing, it's all in mint condition.'

DANCE WITH YOUR ARSE TO THE CEILING. Not a routine often performed in the ballroom but a vivid slice of C19 language.

DASH IN THE BLOOMERS, DO A. I am not sure if the bloomers mentioned are flowers or the long-legged pantaloons fashionable in the 1840s. I suspect it is the clothing.

DEVIL'S BITE. Using contractions of the vaginal muscles to stimulate the penis. The term occurs in Victorian pornography, such as this 1880 effort in the one-handed mag *The Pearl*:

> She bounced up and down on my prick, and now and then rested
> for a moment to indulge in the exquisite pleasure of the devil's bite
> … the folds of her cunt contracting and throbbing upon my
> swelling prick in the most delicious manner.

One wonders if this English lass was blessed with the skills of the Belgian babe in the limerick:

> There was a young lady of Brussels,
> Whose pride were her vaginal muscles;
> She could easily plex them
> And so interflex them
> As to whistle love songs through her bustles.

DIBBLE. An image from gardening that was used in a sexual sense around 1855. (For non-gardeners, a dibble is a pointed tool used to make holes to plant seeds in.)

> Eve was so very curious, she fingered Adam furious,
> Till he dibbled in with might and main his root, root, root;
> Said Eve, 'I do not know, but I think the thing will grow,
> Because I most distinctly felt it shoot, shoot, shoot.'

DICK. An infrequently heard verb from the 1860s; the word usually describes the penis rather than its use.

Dibble

DIDDLE. After an innocent start as a dialect word meaning 'to shake', **diddle** got low down and dirty in the mid-C19 and switched its meaning to copulation.

DIP IT, DIP THE WICK. The wick is rhyming slang (Hampton Wick) and the dipping got under way in the C19.

DIRK. The active life of the Scottish penis from 1620 to 1820. Just one of the aggressive, weapon-based metaphors that sex attracts.

DIVE IN THE DARK. There is an air of derring-do about this sample of C19 chat.

DO A BIT. Sex with a masculine perspective, recorded for the first time in 1860; it is still in use.

DO A PERPENDICULAR. To have sex standing up, in a phrase first recorded about 1860. An interesting variant of the posture appears in verse:

> There was a young lady of Norway
> Who hung by her toes in a doorway,
> Said she to her beau,
> 'Just look at me, Joe,
> I think I've discovered one more way.'

DO ONE'S BUSINESS. In this phrase of the 1860s 'one' always stands for 'her'. The same slang also meant to kill somebody and defecate.

DOCK. In 1560 this had the specific meaning of deflowering a virgin; it became a term for all intercourse and fell out of use by 1840. In C18 underworld slang, 'The cull docked the dell all the darkmans' meant that the gentleman had enjoyed the lady all night long.

DOCKED SMACK-SMOOTH. This describes a man whose **pego** has been amputated because of Cupid's measles or the French pox or some other form of VD.

DOCKING. Jolly jack tars went in for docking. Not parking their ships, but punishing women who displeased them by stripping them before chucking them into the street. OK, it's not actually about sex, but it does show what old customs were about in Merrie England.

DOG, DOGGY FASHION, DOGWAYS. Man copying his best friend by mating on all fours, a term in use from the C17 onwards.

DOG'S MATCH. The full C19 expression is 'make a dog's match of it' and means having sex (in any style) by public highways, carefree as a dog and bitch.

DOG'S RIG. To be at **clicket** until both parties are exhausted and turn their backs on one another in order to sleep. A habit commemorated in slang used in the C18 and C19.

DRAW HIS CORK. A C19 lady's remark when she has exhausted her partner's sexual energy.

DRIVE INTO. A piece of 1870s slang spoken by the man in the partnership.

DRY-BOB. To have intercourse without ejaculating, part of slang from 1750–1850. Or, if you are at Eton College, a cricketer.

DUMB GLUTTON, FEED THE. A household chore a man was expected to attend to at regular intervals in the C18 and the first half of the C19.

DUNKING. Copulation from 1900–1910. Or dipping your biscuit in your tea until it goes soft.

Draw His Cork

EAGLE, RIDE THE. An American expression from the C19 indicating that the lady was mounted on the gentleman. Also recorded as 'fly the eagle'.

EVE'S CUSTOM-HOUSE, ENTER. Bureaucratic imagery from the C18. (See Chapter 2.)

FACE MAKING. The face concerned is that of the child who may be the result of feeding the dumb glutton without taking precautions. The expression was popular in the late C18 and early C19.

FAST-FUCK. Nothing ambiguous about this C19 tarts' slang; the act was rapid and often done standing up.

FAT, BIT OF. Sex with a large partner in 1850 or so.

FEDERATING. A demonstration of how politics can affect slang; the Australian states federated into the Commonwealth of Australia in 1901. And there was a brand-new term for intercourse.

FEEL, HAVE A FEEL, FEEL YOUR WAY TO HEAVEN. These are all ways of describing foreplay from the C18. As a rule they offer the male point of view on operations.

FEET UPPERMOST, LIE WITH. A description of a woman waiting for sex in the missionary position, from the C19 and surviving into the C20.

FEEZE, PHEEZE. Used in the C16 to describe coition, but not since.

FIDDLE. A word whose meaning shifted from foreplay in the C17 to intercourse in the C19.

FINGER, TIP THE LONG FINGER. Casual and unemotional foreplay from the C19.

FIRKYTOODLE. Foreplay according to slangsters from the C17 to the C19; the term is based on a dialect word meaning to beat or strike. Let's leave it before things get sordid.

FISH. A simple C19 description of foreplay's olfactory aspect.

FIT END TO END, FIT ENDS. A practical piece of C19 slang, with no attempt at the fancy poetic stuff.

FLASH IN THE PAN. Intercourse without ejaculation, used from around 1710 onwards; the image is based on gunpowder failing to ignite in a musket's pan.

FLAT-FUCK. A description of lesbian groin contact from the late C19.

FLESH IT. First appearing circa 1550, this dropped out of regular use in the early C20.

FLESH FLUTE, PLAY THE. The same as **bagpipe**, but done outside Scotland.

FLIMP. A C19 word that once meant to hit or smack.

FLOCK OF SPARROWS FLYING OUT OF YOUR ARSE, HAVE A. A colourful Oz-slang way of describing an orgasm, much used in the 1950s.

FLOWERS, EAT HER. Cunnilingus in the C19. Menstrual blood was at times called 'the flowers' so this slang may indicate a special taste in oral sex.

FLUTTER, HAVE A / DO A. Nowadays this means occasional gambling, but in the 1870s it could mean losing one's virginity, having sex for fun not procreation, and being sexually active on a regular basis. A phrase with almost as many uses as a Swiss Army knife.

FOIN. Way back in the C14 this four-letter word meant thrusting with a blade, such as a **dagger**, **dirk** or **sword** (see Chapter 3); by the late C16 it had acquired the sexual implication. **Foin** had disappeared from the language by 1660.

FORAMINATE. A grandiose word that sounds like fornicate with a head cold. It comes from the Latin *foramen*, meaning an orifice, and had a brief vogue in the C17.

FORK, GET ON THE. Part of Victorian slang and based on the term for the vagina, **bit on a fork**.

FOUR-LEGGED FROLIC. The phrase was first recorded in 1850 but Eric Partridge believes it was in use long before that and may be based on a C16 saying, 'There goes more to a marriage than four legs in a bed.' How many divorcing couples wish they'd known that in advance?

Get on the Fork

FRIG. At first this was masturbation, but business expanded to take in screwing.

FUCK. Already discussed in some detail, the word has been with us in print since 1503 and in speech much longer. It began as Standard English but by 1690 was not just slang but unacceptable slang. It is still as active as ever and looks set to remain in rude good health.

FUMBLE. First used to mean foreplay back in the C16 and still going strong, though it is now rather bookish.

FUTTER. Dreamed up by Sir Richard Burton for his erotic translation of *The Thousand and One Nights*, a splendid collection of randy yarns. It wasn't only Aladdin's lamp that got rubbed with surprising results. Burton may have used the French term *foutre* as inspiration.

GAFFER. Not the senior electrician in a film studio but a C19 variant of **chauver**.

GAMAHUCHE. Oral sex in the 1870s to 1890s. In the story *Sub-Umbra* the ever-randy, ever-erect Walter says, 'I stretched Sophie's legs wide apart, and sinking on my knees, gamahuched her virgin cunt.'

Partridge does not include **gamahuche** but does offer the half-sibling gamaruche/gamaroosh, limiting the meaning to fellatio. He thinks the word is derived from French and that the French borrowed it from the Arabs.

GAME, THE FIRST EVER PLAYED. The great sporting tradition of the C19 is commemorated in this healthy-sounding slang. Play up and play the game, you chaps. But what then should we make of the old saying, 'The game's not worth the candle'?

GAME, THE NATIONAL INDOOR. Ludo, snakes and ladders, chess and whist are not celebrated in this late-C19 remark but **nugging** is.

GANCH. In Standard English this means to impale and, in earlier times, was a term from hunting, meaning a wound from a boar's tusk (Venus's lover Adonis was castrated by a wild boar). An informant recalls finding some C19 porn using the term and swears one line went, '"Ganch her oscule afore the Frenchies seize all they can to swive," ejaculated the tar to Midshipman Hardpole.' Research shows that oscule means little mouth. I cannot vouch for this term.

GAY IT. This 1825 expression refers to heterosexual intercourse. **Gay** was used to describe prostitutes and sexually active women. 'Feeling gay' was a way of letting your partner know you were randy.

GET HOME. To induce or experience orgasm, applied from circa 1870.

GET WHAT HARRY GAVE DOLL. From the 1730s into the 1850s women used this expression for intercourse.

GIBLETS. No, not part of a recipe from an C18 Delia Smith, but sex pictured as 'joining giblets'.

GIDDLE. A Scottish name for foreplay, heard ringing down the glens in the C17 and the C18.

GIRL. At Oxford University in the C18 this was a common verb for copulation. Girling was going out and about in search of a girl to **girl**.

GIVE HER/HIM ONE. Plainspoken slang from the latter portion of the C19.

GO FOR IT. A 1920s expression meaning wild and wonderful fornication.

GOAT, PLAY THE. Extremely vigorous lovemaking was compared to the antics of goats.

GOAT'S JIG. In the 1750s a dance that many ladies and gentlemen enjoyed. (The goat was allowed to join in only if it had a nice smile.)

GOBBLE. A term for fellatio going back to the late C18. Grose defined 'a rampant, lustful woman' as a gobble-prick in 1785.

GOOSE. At times in the C19 this was slang for **bottom-fucking**. A good goose at Christmas was considered a great treat in those days.

GOOSE AND DUCK. Rhyming slang from 1855.

GRAVY, GIVE YOUR. In the C19 to achieve orgasm and ejaculation, applied to women as well as men. Remember, it was an article of

Goat's Jig

faith with pornographers of the time that women ejaculated in the same way as men; see *The Pearl* and other C19 porn for references to 'copious spendings'.

GREENS, HAVE/GET YOUR. One of the horticultural metaphors, which became commonplace about 1850–60. A woman ready for sex was said to be 'on for greens'; an eager man was 'after his greens'.

GRIND. The word appeared in the C16 and is usually seen in the phrases 'have a grind' or 'do a grind'.

Give Your Grav

GROWL-BITING. The name of a sexual act derived from the rhyming slang 'growl and grunt'. (See also **tipping the velvet** and **muff-diving**.)

GROWLING. Enjoying a good **grind**; this expression is derived from the C19 rhyming slang for the vagina, **growl** (growl and grunt). In the 1880s a **sailor's pleasure** was defined as 'smoking, yarning, dancing, growling'.

GRUMMET. Either the Royal Navy or the Merchant Navy marooned this slang in English circa 1860.

GUT-STICK, HAVE A BIT OF/TASTE OF. Said by women, according to Partridge. The slang is late C19/early C20.

HANDIE-DANDIE. Taking the name of a children's game, this was used in Scotland from the C16 to the C18. It is sometimes spelled handy-dandy.

HEADS AND TAILS. The 1870s slang for 69.

HEY-GAMMER-COCK, PLAY AT. This is one of those phrases I find it hard to believe was uttered spontaneously by some eager lover. You'd be out of breath before the action started. If **hey-gammer-cock** ever *was* called out, then it was between 1780 and 1880.

HOBBES'S VOYAGE, TO GO ON. The dying words of the philosopher Thomas Hobbes (who described human life as 'nasty, brutish and short') were, 'I am about to take my last voyage, a great leap in the dark.' Sharp slangsters rapidly imported it into their word-hoards. We don't know the name of the great leap he took, but she certainly did for old Tommy. Hobbes handed in his dinner-pail in 1679 and the slang was popular from then until the 1750s.

HOGMAGUNDY. (See **houghmagandie**.)

HOIST. In full this slang, from the 1850s, was in full 'do a hoist in' her or, very rarely, him.

HOLE HER. No frills, no silly emotions, nothing remotely humane about this charmless slang.

HOLE TO HIDE IT IN, GIVE/LEND A MAN A. Coarse even by the standards of C19 lingo.

HOLE-AND-CORNER WORK. The general expression carries a suggestion of furtive, guilty, possibly criminal activity in Standard English; the slang does nothing to dispel that.

HOOPER'S, HIDE HOOPER'S. A distinctly literary effort, being manufactured in 1719 by the writer D'Urfey from a dialect name for the game of hide-and-seek. It has not been used since around 1805.

HORIZONTAL REFRESHMENT. A piece of slang introduced in 1870; in the 1890s it did a reverse of the usual shift and went respectable, if vulgar, and meant eating while seated in a station buffet.

HORIZONTALISE. Partridge describes this as 'low pedantic' and dates the term to 1845.

HORRY. New Zealand C20 slang for **horizontal refreshment**.

HORSE. This cantered into slang in the C17 and has a stud-farm origin, with some stable lad fondly recalling a stallion covering a mare. Who was the first male spectator to turn from the busy beasts to say to a lass, 'Oh, fair maid, I wish I was doing that,' and receive the reply, 'Go ahead, sonny, it's your mare.'

HOT PUDDING FOR SUPPER. Words said by a woman looking forward to a good, hearty meal in the late C19. A similar menu featured 'live sausage for dinner'.

HOT ROLL WITH CREAM. Another favourite dish on the C19 menu.

HOUGHMAGANDIE. A braw Scots word that sounds randy and riotous. Burns used it in *The Merry Muses of Caledonia* during the 1790s:

> The mair ye bang, the mair she squeals,
> An' hey for houghmagandie.

HOW'S-YER-FARVER. The full phrase is 'a bit o' how's-yer-farver' (father) and began its career as part of a music-hall act during the First World War. Like **nookie** people thought of it as vulgar rather than obscene.

HUDDLE. In C17 dialect, a cuddle; in the C18 slang, a **fuck**.

HUFFLE. The C18 version of **bagpiping** (oral sex) or, according to modern authorities, having sex with your partner's armpit.

HUMP. This was fashionable in Britain circa 1760; by 1785 Grose considered it out of date. About 1800 **hump** was exported to the USA and has been returned to us in recent years. NB: the Australian phrase 'humping your bluey' does not indicate unnatural relations with a backpack (bluey in Oz-slang).

IMPALE. A writerly kind of word that was used in the C19 a lot. It is still hanging about the place today.

IN-AND-IN, PLAY AT. One of the literary types of couplings that D'Urfey noted in the C17.

IN-AND-OUT. A variation on the previous name, usually in the shape 'play at in-and-out' and more street speak than literary.

INDORSE. A term for sodomy from circa 1780, making a pun on the old word for back – dorse.

IRISH TOOTHACHE, GIVE A HOT POULTICE FOR. In full this is 'give a hot poultice for the Irish toothache' and was used by women from circa 1860.

IRISH WHIST, PLAY AT. An unusual card game from 1740, with a pack stripped down to knaves and queens.

IRRUMATION. A highfalutin Victorian word for a **blow job**.

ITCH-BUTTOCKS, PLAY. Another of those olde worlde sports that have departed. Either that or a coarse expression indicating copulation, noted by the author John Florio in 1598.

JAPE. This word has enjoyed a mixed career. It was around in the C14, when it described seduction or trickery. Chaucer's Pardoner fools gullible priests and worshippers with 'feyned flaterye and japes', making them believe stew bones are those of saints.

By 1600 it was considered unsavoury and disappeared into the black hole reserved for unwashed and unwanted words. In the late C19 it came sneaking out but disguised as a practical joke or prank played by schoolboys.

JAZZ, JASS. The whole of an original, inventive, hilarious, tragic, gutsy and tender music takes its name from a word used in the American South for another activity that is gutsy, tender, hilarious, etc. In 1927 the US *Journal of Abnormal and Social Psychology* made the sniffy comment: 'The word ... used both as a verb and as a noun to denote the sex act ... has long been a common vulgarity ...' Well, if that's the way you feel, you ain't gettin' none o' my sweet jellyroll.

JIG, DANCE THE FEATHERBED. A domestic ballet, generally a *pas de deux* of unspec- ified duration and no standard performance level. The slang premiered in the C17.

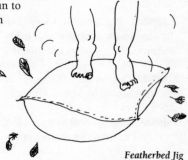

Featherbed Jig

JIG-A-JIG, JIG-JIG. Taken from the chorus of a broadsheet ballad of the 1840s, 'Jig Jig to the Hirings'. The variant jiggy-jig was peculiar to the Indian Army; it is said that Indian women climaxing would call out the word.

JIGGLE. Sexual intercourse in slang from circa 1845; a main feature was the work of the 'jiggling-stick'.

JOB, DO A WOMAN'S JOB FOR HER. The word and the phrase became popular round about 1850. Both carry the implication that the woman was pleased by the man's efforts.

JOBBING. A sample of slang from Scotland that was first used in the C17 and is still heard in the C21.

JOCK, JOCKING. Names in use from the C17 until 1900, though **jocking** was still used in parts of Scotland up to the 1960s. A girl who **jocked** too often with too many men was called a Scotch warming-pan in 1860.

JOCKUM-CLOY. The **jockum** part is the penis; the cloy is thieves' slang for a robber or burglar and the whole expression came into being in the C16. It had disappeared by the early decades of the C19.

JOLT. Another of the striking/hitting slang terms that were popular in the C19.

JOTTLE. A forgotten word from the C19, when it appeared most often in forms like 'do a jottle' and 'go jottling'. Records of the expeditions were written on jottling-pads, of course.

JUMBLE. The author D'Urfey noted the existence of the word in the 1670s when it was already a century old. It has long been out of use, so don't get excited when you see posters advertising a jumble sale near you.

JUMM. One more of the words Thomas Urquhart thought up for his translation of Rabelais in the 1680s. A literary oddity rather than slang.

JUMP. This appeared in the C16, often as 'jump up and down on' and 'give a jump to'. Still heard today, mainly in the north of England.

KEG, LITTLE BIT OF. Partridge defines this as 'human copulation' and dates it to 1909.

KEIFER. A word for intercourse possibly morphed from an Arabic term meaning 'the amiable beauty of a woman'.

KIND, ACT OF KIND. The origin is obscure and the use is polite and disguising. The term seems to have been concocted about 1845.

KIPPLES. Slang from the C19 and usually found as 'dance kipples'. It may be connected to kip, meaning a brothel, or perhaps a poor pronunciation of couples.

KNEE, BREAK HER. To deflower a virgin or to make any woman pregnant in C19 speak.

KNEE-TREMBLER. Sex standing up, often with the overtone of furtive haste. The useful term dates from 1850.

KNOB. The slang, generally used by a man about a woman in the form 'knob her', is late C19, becoming more frequently used in the late C20.

KNOCK. A striking image from 1580 that has survived until the present day, though generally in the shape of a knocking shop (brothel). A knocker is somebody skilled at knocking, of course. To make life easier such people wear knocking jackets (nightshirts) to bed. **Knock** is related to **nock** and **notch** (see Chapter 2). The American term knocked up, meaning pregnant, originated in the C19.

LADIES' TAILORING. In 1815 some slangmonger considered **stitch** (see below) and extrapolated from that. **Ladies' tailoring** did not secure a commanding and lasting place in the fashion stakes.

LAP-CLAP. Between 1650 and 1750 this slang named the pleasures of intercourse followed by the sorrows of conception.

LARKING. Cunnilingus in the middle of the C18. Captain Grose included the word in the first edition of his dictionary then dropped it. No one knows why.

LEAP. First recorded with a sexual meaning in the C18, **leap** has been used to describe a stallion mounting a mare.

LEATHER. A sample of 1930s slang for heterosexual anal intercourse.

LEG OVER, LEG ON, LAY A LEG ON. Leg over has a modern sound and has become increasingly popular in the past thirty years, so it may come as a surprise to learn it was used in the 1760s, like **leg on** and **lay a leg on**. They may all be linked to an old phrase 'she has broken her leg', i.e. given birth to a bastard.

LERRICOMPOOP. A rare word from the C16 that may be a twisting of lerricomtwang, meaning a fool.

LEVEL-COIL. Based on a loud, rough game played during the C17, whose rules I have been unable to trace. Anyone out there know the moves?

LICK-SPIGOT. A spigot being a tap (or turn-cock) you can work out that this C17 slang meant fellatio and the woman performing the act. Lick-twat was a cruder word for the same person and not a man who provided oral sex for a woman.

LIFT LEG, PLAY AT. A popular sport from 1700–1850, also appearing as 'lift your leg'.

LIGHT THE LAMP. Supposedly said by women from the 1880s; it may be a literary term rather than slang.

LING-GRAPPLING. Intercourse or heavy petting in the argot of the 1890s. The ling is a large fish much like a cod. (See also chapters 2 and 6.)

LOSE THE MATCH AND POCKET THE STAKES. A woman's comment on copulation from the start of the C19.

MAKE FEET FOR CHILDREN'S STOCKINGS. A sober and prescient Victorian expression.

MAKE THE CHIMNEY SMOKE. Giving a woman an orgasm from the 1850s onwards. The phrase is no longer used in this era of central heating.

MAN. Copulation from the male point of view and part of slang from circa 1890.

MATTRESS JIG. A lively dance much in favour in the C18 and C19.

MEAT, HAVE A PIECE OF. At first, back in the C16, meat was slang for the entire human body; by the 1690s it meant the vagina or penis and in 1720 **meat** stood for copulation. The word was adapted for a number of uses; a 'bit of meat' was a whore and using her services, for which you paid the 'price of meat' (C18); somebody 'fond of meat' was randy (C19) and 'meat and drink' was a date featuring booze and bonking (C19–C20).

MELTING MOMENTS. Slang for a fat couple fornicating from 1810 to 1890. Gad, what energy!

MERRY BOUT. A term for coition used from 1780–1830.

MINETTE. Fellatio for the toffs of the 1850s to the 1870s; Walter mentions an encounter with a young man and becoming 'engrossed with minetting his doodle'. He adds that the chap failed to 'irruminate me with skill', which is hard luck.

MINK, FUCK LIKE A. An Australian term for enthusiastic sexual activity.

MOLLY PEATLEY'S JIG. The lady's ID is unknown – Eric Partridge speculates she was a prostitute (a moll) surnamed Peatley – but her dance was popular from the C18 until the early years of the C19. Since when it has gone on under other names.

Fuck Like a Mink

MOLROWING. An obscure verb for **futtering** that enjoyed a brief vogue during the 1860s.

MOST OF YOU. A cheery catchphrase for intercourse from 1850, the full version being 'all there but the most of you'. Perhaps a comment from a disappointed lady?

MOUNT. An old term to describe all kinds of other animals mating, but not applied to human beings until the C16. The verb is still in use.

MOW. Scottish and North Country dialect going back to the early C16, but not much heard in the past two centuries.

MUFF-DIVING. Oral sex, male to female; a C19 expression that is more often heard in Australia and the USA than Great Britain. Or so I have been told.

MUTTON. The word's meaning changed from a harlot to the vagina and then to sexual intercourse. The viewpoint is male, i.e. 'he'll be in her mutton' or 'he's fond of his mutton'.

MUTTON FOR BEEF. In the C19 women said they gave **mutton for beef** to describe intercourse.

NASTY. An American term from the 1950s and 1960s; Frank Zappa sang about 'doin' a nasty on the White House lawn' in 1967.

NAUGHTY. From circa 1850 'do the naughty' meant going on the game, whoring, and applied to women only. The phrase do a/have a naughty, or its abbreviation naughties, are C19 and C20 Australian slang.

NEBUCHADNEZZAR. The full 1860s expression is 'take Nebuchadnezzar out to grass'. Why? Because in the Bible Nebuchadnezzar ate grass, i.e. was fond of his greens. The slang also means exposing the penis in the open air – thus exposing the organ to possible public ridicule. (See Chapter 3.)

NEST, TO BE ON THE. Slang created in the late C18 and still heard in the late C20. Considered somewhat literary or saloon bar by many.

NIBBLE. The use of sexual intercourse as a food substitute is suggested by this mid-C19 expression.

NICK. A word first used about 1550 for cheating or conning people; it gained the sexual dimension in the C18.

NIGGLE, NIGGLING. We go all the way back to 1565 with this one; **niggling** could mean spending time with a woman, as well as having sex, and there is a strong hint that the company was paid for, a niggler being a harlot.

NIGHT-PHYSIC. Medicine for those long, dark hours when comfort is required. The expression used was 'S/he serves him/her night-physic'. The slang-dispenser first mixed it up about 1680 but then withdrew the prescription about 1710.

NIGHT-WORK. Same thing as **night-physic** but without the medicinal qualities.

NIGHTINGALE, LISTENING TO THE. A fancy expression for sexual shenanigans in the C16 and C17.

NOCK. The writer John Florio used the word in the 1590s and derived it from notch, so it is not simply a poor spelling of **knock**. Sometimes **nock** is used to name the **quim**.

NODGE. I have seen this called a C17 word for sex but cannot trace it. The nearest is a word for a fool: nodgecock. That sounds as though it could have a sexual element so I'll leave **nodge** in.

NOOKIE, NOOKY. Partridge believes this C19 and C20 word is middle-class, genteel and semi-respectable. It is based on the Standard English nook, meaning hole.

> A very smart lady called Cookie
> Said, 'I like to mix gambling with nookie,
> Before every race
> I go back to my place
> And curl up with a very good bookie.'

NUB. Fornication in the language of the C18 and C19; the word is linked to the dialect terms for a protuberance and to shake or jog. In underworld slang **nub** means neck, and nubbing could be sex or execution by hanging. Well, orgasm has been called 'the little death', so go for the big 'un, kid.

NUGGING. This word is probably taken from nudge. From 1750–1850 it was used in the expression nugging-cove, a man on pleasure bent, who might well find it in a nugging-ken (a brothel).

OYSTER, CATCH AN. A phrase used by women (oyster meaning both semen and vagina) in the C19.

PALLIARDISE. This could be based on the idea of lying down on a palliasse, a straw-stuffed mattress. (Palliasse also indicated a cheap whore, presumably from her place of work.)

PAUNCHES, JOIN. A cheery C18 image of mighty bellies bouncing together, like figures in a Hogarth or Rowlandson drawing.

PEG. A word that enjoyed brief popularity in the 1850s; peg more often meant a drink than intercourse.

PERFORATE. yet another example of sexual aggression from the Victorian age.

PHYSIC. In the C17 this was the same as night-physic but taken during daylight hours. The author Massinger wrote of a certain lady, 'She sends for her young doctor/Who ministers physic to her on her back.' You can't get that on the NHS. Yet.

Join Paunche

PICKLE-ME-TICKLE-ME, PLAY AT. Harmless fun in the C17, except for unwanted pregnancies, angry fathers, the pox, etc.

PILE-DRIVING. An industrial metaphor used in the C19. Very butch and masterful.

PIPE. Simple C19 slang.

PIZZLE. A male term, usually given as 'pizzle her'. The word may be descended from the Flemish *pezel* or the Low German *pesel*, both of which mean 'little sinew'. (See Chapter 3.)

PLANT A MAN/WOMAN. A gardening aspect of copulation, first recorded around 1650 and not considered slang, though certainly not a polite usage. It had become slang by 1705.

Plant a Man

PLATE, PLATING. A sample of rhyming slang, being short for 'plate of ham' meaning gam, which itself was a short version of the old term for oral sex, **gamahuche**. The light horseshoes worn by racehorses are called plates; if you're at Newmarket, Ascot or Aintree, keep calm when you hear about a filly or stallion being plated.

PLAY DADDIES AND MUMMIES/FATHERS AND MOTHERS. Rather sick-making baby talk created early in the C20 and still clinging to life.

PLAY WITH YOUR ACE. The ace here is the **ace of spades** (vagina; see Chapter 2) and the slang is from the C19. It also occurs as 'play the ace against the jack'.

PLOUGH A FURROW. An old country labour – happens all the time in *The Archers* – which C19 slangmasters adapted for their needs.

PLOW THE BACK FORTY. Based on American agricultural habits and, I am assured, meaning vaginal rather than anal intercourse. A late-C19 and early-C20 phrase.

PLOWTER. Coition in an old English dialect; the word originally referred to splashing through mud.

PLUCK A ROSE. In sexual slang (and poetry) this indicates defloration and has done since the C16. To women in the C18 the phrase meant urinating.

PLUG. Copulation reduced to a different four-letter word for a change in the C18. In the 1960s the word meant anal sex.

PLUMBING. A little-used term from the early C20. The author Arnold Bennett considered this limerick featuring it the best ever written:

> There was a young plumber of Leigh
> Who was plumbing a maid by the sea;
> Said the maid, 'Cease your plumbing,
> I think someone's coming,'
> Said the plumber, still plumbing, 'It's me.'

POKE. Simple, unadorned C19 slang for simple folk. Another word that has proved long-lasting.

POLKA, DANCE THE MATRIMONIAL. The polka was *the* dance of the 1840s and the slangsters were quick to make use of it. The phrase was often reduced to simply 'the m.p.'

POOP, POOP-NODDY. The sexual act and a low-decibel fart in both the C17 and the C18.

POP IT IN. No-frills C19 invitation to sex.

PRACTISE IN THE MILKY WAY. Playing with a woman's breasts according to the slang of the 1630s.

PRATLEY'S GIG. This is considered by historians to be a variation of **Molly Peatley's jig**.

PRAY WITH THE KNEES UPWARDS. A female comment on sex in the missionary position; Grose recorded it in 1785.

PRICK THE GARTER, PLAY AT. An C18 pastime, which took its name from a rigged gambling game 'prick in the garter/loop'.

PRICK-CHINKING. A name for copulation used in the first half of the C18.

PRONG. Chiefly an American term and active from 1860 onwards. The word began to gain popularity in the UK about a century later.

PUDDING. One simple word does duty for penis, semen and pregnancy. D'Urfey recorded it in 1682. To be in the Pudding Club, meaning pregnant, is C19 slang and is short for a lady being caught with 'a bellyful of marrow-pudding'.

PULLY-HAULY, PLAY AT. This C18 expression sounds somewhat nautical to me, like an order that Nelson or John Paul Jones might have bawled out from the quarterdeck.

PUMP. One of the less imaginative pieces of slang thought up in the C18.

PUNCH. Defloration in the C18 and early C19. According to Ned Ward, a 'punchable nun' was a whore. Repeated deflowerings were the speciality of some prostitutes, who repaired the damage surgically or by using a powerful alum solution called pucker-water.

PURSER'S GRIND. An expression used by women for good sex with a very well-endowed male, heard from circa 1850 onwards. The purser or pusser is in charge of a ship's stewards, food supplies, etc., and is seen either as mean (a purser's dip is a very small candle) or the source of all good things.

PUSH-PIN. In 1623 Massinger used the expression, 'She would never tell/Who played at push-pin with her' and in 1707 Ned Ward recorded the variation push-pike.

PUT. Created in the late C19, this is most often found in the phrases 'do a put' and 'have a put-in'.

PUT, PLAY AT TWO-HANDED. A popular expression in the late C18, but long since forgotten.

QUIMMING. After **quim** (see Chapter 2) and, in the C19 when it was first noted, often associated with such low companions as quim-wedging and quim-sticking.

RAM. A shepherd's delight, using the **ramrod** in the 1830s.

RANTUM-SCANTUM. A drumbeat of an expression for intercourse that clattered into life in the C18. It calls for a pounding of kettledrums and loyal soldiers bellowing, 'Tow-row-row for the British grenadiers!' as an accompaniment.

RASP. A seldom-met verb for copulation dating from the mid-Victorian period. The commoner form was 'do a rasp', and both sound painful, bringing thoughts of large, coarse files wielded by large, coarse people.

RATTLE. One of the popular words for intercourse in the middle of the C19.

REEL OF BOGIE. One of those charming old Scottish country dances, I believe, featuring wild capers and hoots of joy.

RIDE. Respectable as a bishop in the Middle Ages, but by the C18 considered to be low, vulgar and not a word to take a dish of tea with in the best drawing rooms.

RIFFLE. Handling a man's privates to get him randy. Derives from a cardsharping term for a crooked shuffle.

RIFLE. A word from the ancient sport of falconry describing the mating of hawks; the tercel (cock) **rifles** the falcon (hen). The slang for human coupling first took wing in the C17.

Chimes

RIM, RIMMING. Oral sex involving tongue-to-anus contact. The actress Maureen Lipman's remark comes to mind: 'You know the worst thing about oral sex? The view.'

RING, ASK FOR THE. This was a request for anal intercourse uttered during the 1950s.

RING HER/HIS BELL. To bring a partner to orgasm, in C19 words. A more genteel version substitutes chimes for bell.

Ring My Be

ROAST DUCK. A fowl piece of rhyming slang from the first half of the C20.

ROAST ON A SPIT, SPIT ROAST. This means a woman fellating one man while another enters her from the rear. An expression based on the old method of cooking joints of meat, whole lambs, oxen, etc. on long metal spits thrust through the body from stem to stern. Currently practised (allegedly) by certain Premiership footballers.

ROGER. Captain Grose's dictionary states that this comes 'From the name Roger, frequently given to a bull' (1785) and other experts claim it was the name of the town bull in the Middle Ages, i.e. the bull kept to service all local cows as a public service.

However, it may be the creation of a gentleman from Virginia, USA, one William Byrd of Westover, whose *Secret Diary, 1709–1712* always uses **roger** for intercourse with his spouse, e.g. Christmas Day, 1711, 'I rogered her lustily'. One wonders which of the pair enjoyed that Christmas present most.

It is impossible to leave this entry without quoting the limerick about a randy Roger:

> There was a young maid of Cape Cod,
> Who thought babies were fashioned by God,
> But 'twas not the Almighty
> Who hoiked up her nightie –
> 'Twas Roger the lodger, the sod.

ROUST. Found in the late C16, e.g. in Hall's *Satires* he writes of a lady who 'seeks her third roust on silent toes'. I suppose the last two words mean she was sneaking about and don't describe what she planned to roust with. But perhaps this is the first toe-job in English literature.

RUB BELLY. Not a much-used slang term but it has had its friends in the two hundred years since it first appeared.

RUB OFF. Coition from the C17 to the early C19. Sometimes the slang meant masturbation but **rub up** was more often used (see Chapter 6).

RUMBUSTICATE. This swashbuckling substitute for copulation swaggered on to the stage about 1880 but was yesterday's slang by 1910. It was the bastard issue of rumbustical (unruly) and a Cornish dialect word spiflicate (beat or thrash or amaze).

In Cambridge in the 1660s a potent cocktail called rambooze was made, consisting of ale, eggs, wine and sugar (the winter version) and milk, wine, rosewater and sugar for summer slurping. A few tankards of rambooze made everyone ready to **rumbusticate**.

RUMP. Doggy-style mating, according to this name from the middle of the C19.

RUMP-WORK. A term for intercourse used from 1860–1914. It has commercial overtones, as a rumper was a prostitute.

RUT. Not truly slang but a basic term for the mating of all animals. It is here as an excuse to include this limerick:

> An unfortunate lad from Calcutta
> Vibrated all through from his stutter;
> To eat, walk or speak
> He would shake for a week,
> But he was awfully good as a rutter.

SAILOR'S PLEASURE. This consisted of story-telling, smoking and **growling**, according to a definition of the 1880s.

Sailor's Pleasure

SALLENGER'S ROUND. The name of a country dance, a bawdy song and a **fuck** in the C17.

SALT. Rogering in the language of the late C17 and early C18.

SARD. An ancient term found in the translation of the Gospels in the famous Lindisfarne Gospels made in the 7C, with extra glosses in the C10. Like many other words **sard** fell from favour and was banished to the realm of slang in the C16.

SCOUR. Copulation from roughly 1770 to 1850 and much used in its early days, when it could be spelled scower or scowre.

SCREW. The sexual meaning entered the language in the C18, but it also meant a broken-down old horse, a robbery carried out with a skeleton key, a miser and to glance at somebody. In the early C19 screw crossed the Atlantic and made itself at home in the USA. Sometimes the word appears in colourful phrases, e.g. 'screw her sideways to Christmas' and 'screw the arse off'. It features, too, in the carpenter's dream of a woman: 'flat as a board and easy to screw'. In the elaborate poetry the Vikings enjoyed composing, a woman might sometimes be called a beer-plank.

SCROUPERISE. Originally the word indicated rubbing against something; from 1650–1750 the something was a portion of the opposite sex.

SHAG. The act of love and also the lovers (especially the man) involved in it, according to Grose's admirable dictionary of 1785, which offers this quote to illustrate the use: 'He is but bad shag.' The slang is from a dialect word meaning shake. In the C20 it became slang for wanking (see Chapter 6).

> I don't like to see, coming out of Cremorne,
> A girl with her muslin much crumpled and torn,
> Arm in arm with a fellow who'd had the mishap
> To forget, when he shagged her, to button his flap.

The Cremorne Pleasure Gardens were a popular place to go in the 1840s, as this Victorian ditty suggests.

SHAKE. A word linked to shag but dating back to the 1580s as sexual slang.

SHIFT SERVICE. This slang reduces sex to an industrialised, rationalised, factory-work process and dates from the C19.

SHOOT. What happens to give you the wet part of a wet dream, circa 1870.

SHOOT BETWEEN WIND AND WATER. An anatomically minded slangster of the 1680s concocted this vivid phrase.

SHOOT IN THE TAIL. A C19 phrase meaning both copulation and sodomy.

SHOOT LONDON BRIDGE. In the C18 the boatmen on the Thames would demonstrate their skills by shooting the rapids under London Bridge. The courage, balance, guile and craft needed made the feat worthy of acting as slang for fucking.

SHOOT OVER THE STUBBLE. Premature ejaculation given a sporting look in the C18.

SHOOT YOUR MILT, SHOOT YOUR ROE. In C19 these were terms for ejaculation.

SHOOT YOUR WAD. One more term for a seminal discharge, this one popular in the USA from the 1920s onwards.

SHOT, GIVE HER A. A simple C18 instruction.

SHOT IN THE LOCKER, STILL HAVE. A male's claim to be potent, first recorded about 1880.

SHOVE. Yet again the Victorian age provides a simple, unfeeling description of sex from the man's point of view:

> One day we rode into the market-town, and, putting up our horses, strolled about. Fred said, 'Let's both go and have a shove.' 'Where are the girls?' said I.

SHTUP. An ancient Yiddish term for intercourse. Fans of the film *Blazing Saddles* will remember the saloon singer Lily von Shtup. They may also recollect the town in which everyone was called Johnson and the bartender had the misfortune to be Anal Johnson.

SKIRT, DO A BIT OF. An early-C20 description of screwing.

Do a Bit of Skirt

SLICE OF HAM. Another rhyming slang for 'gam' (gamahuche). (See **plate**.)

SLIP HER A LENGTH. A phrase from the C19 for heterosexual sex that is frequently used today. A woman at a party I attended in 2001 responded to a drunken man's offer with 'You're long on promise and short on a length to slip anyone.' He was her ex-husband, so she'd know. In Australia the slang was 'slip him a length' and strictly gay.

SMOKE. Copulation in the C17, after Sir Walter Raleigh made it home from the Americas with the baccy.

SNABBLE. A country word meaning overeating, applied by C19 slangsters to greedy coition.

SNUG. This word for rutting has connotations of warm, cosy feelings and rooms and being 'snug as a bug in a rug'. It dates from the late C19.

SOFT FOR HARD, GIVE. Another example of the Victorian female giving to the male in slang's sexual wonderland.

SPARROW CATCHING. In prostitutes' slang of the 1880s this meant patrolling the streets in search of customers. Back in the Middle Ages the sparrow was renowned for its lechery and ceaseless fornication, according to Chaucer. (See Chapter 8 for a Roman view of the manly little bird.)

SPIDER CLAW. This somewhat sinister expression simply meant holding and stroking the testicles and was popular about a century ago. As in this joke:

> Q: If I have a mothball in my left and a mothball in my right hand, what have I got?
> A: The undivided attention of a very large moth.

SPLIT. A very basic image for intercourse from the C18.

SPLIT MUTTON. Slang for the penis and coition from approximately 1650–1850.

SPREAD, DO A. The expression goes back to 1840 and is slang at its most literal, from the female point of view.

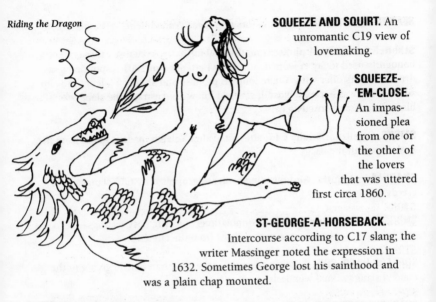

Riding the Dragon

SQUEEZE AND SQUIRT. An unromantic C19 view of lovemaking.

SQUEEZE-'EM-CLOSE. An impassioned plea from one or the other of the lovers that was uttered first circa 1860.

ST-GEORGE-A-HORSEBACK. Intercourse according to C17 slang; the writer Massinger noted the expression in 1632. Sometimes George lost his sainthood and was a plain chap mounted.

ST GEORGE RIDING THE DRAGON. Sex with the woman sitting astride the man, as named by slangsters from the C17 to the C19. The position was also called 'George upon the dragon' and was believed to be the best way to make sure of conceiving a son who'd become a bishop. I doubt if that thought was uppermost in the minds of *The Pearl*'s merry rutters in 1880:

> She was persuaded to ride a St George upon me and my cock was inserted in her tender cunt and allowed slowly to get into position; but the excitement was too great for me and I shot a stream of sperm up her …

No control, some fellows.

STAB IN THE THIGH. Although this sounds like a painful experience with a penknife, it is no more than late-C19 to early-C20 slang for intercourse.

STAND-UP. Same thing as a **knee-trembler** and recorded first circa 1850.

STANDING ROOM FOR A MAN, STANDING ROOM FOR ONE ONLY. Green's *Slang Down the Ages* says this is a term women use rather than men. It came into use in the C19 and slangmongers coined 'understandings' to mean the woman's conquests. (See Chapter 2.)

STAR GAZING, GO. An early C19 saying that suggests the lady found not much else of interest to do while beneath the gentleman.

STITCH. Grose's dictionary defines this as 'a tailor', adding 'Also a term for lying with a woman'.

STOAT, FUCK LIKE A. This was C19 praise for a lover.

STORY. Professional talk from ladies of the night; 'do the story with him' means sex with a paying client and was written down as such in 1734.

STRADDLE. A bookish kind of term, perhaps not really slang but a literary euphemism from the end of the C19.

STRAP, STRAPPING. Heterosexual intercourse in the C17 and onwards. From about 1870 the Standard English idea of strapping as a large, active, vigorous person took over.

STROKE, TAKE A. This was recorded in 1780 and is used by a man of a woman.

STROP YOUR BEAK. Here beak means penis. It is from the late C19 and no longer in regular use.

STRUM. The music lover's choice of word from circa 1780, when eager young lute-players twiddled their pegs and thought of having a long, hard pluck.

STUFF. Partridge's *Dictionary of Historical Slang* says this 1850s verb is taken from the upholstery trade; it is widely used today, though often in the derisive form 'Get stuffed!'

SUMMER CABBAGE, HAVE SOME. An elaborate (and seasonal) C19 way of saying you are getting your greens.

SUPPER, GIVE A MAN HIS SUPPER. This late-C19 phrase is sometimes given a more intimate flavour by offering the supper to 'the old man' (husband). A woman sitting in front of the fire with her skirts raised was said to be 'warming the old man's supper'.

SWITCH, SWITCHEL. From the 1660s and linking sex to the use of the switch, meaning a small whip. By some odd quirk of linguistics, in Newfoundland the word for cold tea is *switchel*.

SWIVE. One of the grand old words, all the way back to 1440, and, like **fuck**, was respectable for several centuries. By 1800 it had become a literary term, only used 'self-consciously' by writers. The goddess Venus was called the Queen of Swiveland.

Lord Rochester wrote one of his acerbic verses claiming: 'I've swived more whores more ways than Sodom's walls/E'er knew ...' The exact number his lordship was boasting of is unknown.

TAIL. The first use of this word to mean intercourse was in the C18; the use spread to America and Australia and returned to us in the C20 as the American expression 'piece of tail'. (For more information see the entry in Chapter 2.) A heavy-handed C19 joke (reports Jonathon Green) was 'make a settlement in tail', with a pun on the legal term entail.

TAKE COCK. Borrowed from West Country dialect in the late C19 and employed in parts of the Cotswolds until the 1970s.

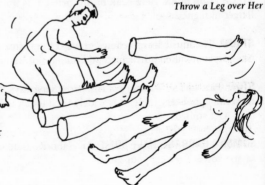

Throw a Leg over Her

TAKE THE STARCH OUT OF. A woman's way of saying she has sexually exhausted a man.

THROW A LEG OVER HER. This expression suggests athletics in the bedchamber about 1780.

THRUM. A C17 term based on playing a stringed instrument such as a lute.

THUMB. A popular activity in the C18 that saw the **thumb of love** properly employed and out of mischief.

THUMBUGGER. Exactly what it sounds like. Walter (who else?) recorded a threesome with himself, a young man and a particularly demanding young woman. She **took the starch out of them** but wanted more, so: 'I licked her bum then thrust my thumb into it, took his balls in my other hand and thumbuggered her while I squeezed his cods.'

TIP THE LONG 'UN. Farmer and Henley's massive dictionary of slang defines this expression as 'To foraminate a woman', and places it in the 1890s.

TITTIE-OGGIE, TITTY-OGGIE. Fellatio in the C19 and the C20.

TOM. North Country slang commenting on the behavioural likeness of the human and feline male.

TONYGLE. In the C16 this term was formed by running together the words 'to' and 'niggle'. It did not have a lengthy career.

TOUCH UP. Multi-role slang meaning heavy petting (C18–C20); then sexual intercourse (late 1700s to c.1850) and masturbation (C19 onwards).

TOWZE. Copulation, so described from circa 1600 to 1750.

TREAD. In poultry-breeding circles this is the term for a cock mounting a hen. Slangsters modified it to **chuck a tread** about 1865.

TROLLEY AND TRUCK. Rhymes with **fuck**, of course, and was part of the rhyming slang lexicon in the early c20.

TROMBONING, GO. This was a favourite hobby of many in the 1880s; the action of the trombone's slide inspired the slangmakers of the day.

TUMBLE. Used by Shakespeare and many others before and after. In the C19 it was modified to 'do a tumble'; a related expression was 'tumble-in', short for 'tumble into bed'.

TUP. For the shepherd this described the ram coupling with the ewe; it could also be applied to cows and bulls before it was extended to humans. The word was first recorded in the C16.

TURN UP, TURN UP YOUR TAIL. Both phrases were used by women when talking about intercourse; both originated in the C17 and were in use until the mid-C18.

Under Petticoating

UNDER PETTICOATING. It is rare for clothing to be mentioned in sex slang (apart from the modern 'get into her pants'); this C19 expression is a reminder that women once wore many layers of clothing and a chap had to be handy with a hook-and-eye, not to mention a corset lace. A slightly different version is to 'go up her petticoats'.

UP HER WAY. A phrase from the 1890s that enjoyed a brief vogue.

UP TAILS ALL. A sweet C17 expression based on a popular song. Fans of *Wind in the Willows* may recall Ratty's song 'Ducks' Ditty' that had this expression as a chorus, and ponder the matter.

VELVET, TIP THE. Defined in a dictionary of 1698 as 'to tongue a woman', the slang was in use until the early C20; in recent years a novel and its television adaptation have revived the expression. Some pornographers of the late C19 used **tip the velvet** to mean kissing with tongues as well as cunnilingus.

WAMES, NAIL TWA WAMES TEGITHER. *Wame* is Scots for stomach, so you join up the dots of this one for yourself.

WAP. A C17 term for tupping based on a dialect word meaning to knock down. A 'wap-apace mort' was a sexually enthusiastic and experienced woman. It was underworld slang and became part of a rogues' proverb: 'If she won't wap for a win, let her trine for a make' – 'If she won't lie with a man for a penny, let her hang for a halfpenny.' Like some other underworld expressions, Timberlake Wertenbaker revived the proverb in her 1988 play *Our Country's Good*.

WHACK IT UP. Another of the C19's striking images of fornication – they did think a lot about punishment when taking their pleasures. In the sense of a powerful punch or blow, whack existed in several dialects in the C18.

WHAM-BAM, THANK YOU, MA'AM. An American phrase for a quickie, first recorded in the late C19.

WIND THE CLOCK. This has a literary origin. In Laurence Sterne's 1759 novel *Tristram Shandy* Mrs Shandy asks her husband if he's wound the clock just as little Tristram is conceived. The slang was first recorded in 1760.

WINDWARD PASSAGE, NAVIGATE THE. Anal intercourse, according to a nautically minded slangmonger of the 1780s. The phrase was short-lived.

WRIGGLE NAVELS. This sounds rather jolly and became part of the lexicon in about 1750; it was still in use during the last century. An uncomfortable phrase suggesting over-indulgence was 'gall the navel'.

YODEL UP THE CANYON. An informant tells me this was C19 and early-C20 Services (especially the Royal Navy) slang for cunnilingus; it was borrowed from the US Navy. Variants include 'yodel in the canyon of love' and 'yodel up the valley'.

ZIGZIG. This, on the other hand, is well-known Services jargon and used by the British forces in the Mediterranean, Middle East and India in the late C19 and C20. It is probably the bastard child of **jig-jig**.

6. GALLOP YOUR MAGGOT

Soon after my return from Leyden I was recommended by good Master Bates to be surgeon of the Swallow.

Jonathan Swift: *Gulliver's Travels*

What is it about masturbation that gets so many people hot under the collar? (Apart from the excitement and physical effort, that is.) Self-stimulation is enjoyable, does not cause insanity, hairy palms or seriously weaken the system. As the sex therapist and counsellor Anne Hooper has pointed out in her book *The Body Electric*, masturbation beats the hell out of cocoa, soap operas and early nights.

The negative image begins with the word's possible origin, the Latin phrase *manu stuprare,* meaning to defile by hand, which does not indicate great affection. However, it may be linked to *masturbari,* a word of unknown origin. Further loathing was thrust on masturbation by religious and moral dictators, whose fundamental theory seems to have been: 'If it's nice, it must be wrong.' As religion has been mentioned, let's clear up the misunderstanding about poor old Onan, whose name has been given to generations of tossers. His sad tale is found in *Genesis*, chapter 38, verses 8–9. Onan's 'sin' was not masturbation; he was forced to marry his brother's widow and, rather than get her pregnant, he pulled out and came on the ground. For which, like his brother, Onan was slain by Jehovah.

In the eighteenth and nineteenth centuries learned medical men wrote fat books on the dangers and evils of this most unnatural of vices, while the clergy made sure everyone knew that the habit blasted your soul to the deepest pit. One such book, from 1724, was called *The Crime of Onan, together with that of his Brother Er, Punished with Sudden Death, or the Heinous Vice of Self-defilement with all its Dismal Consequences*. Those indulging in the habit shortened their lives, reduced their physical and mental strength, and were prone to blindness, cretinism, eternal damnation, drooling, hairy palms, feeble legs and bent spines.

After an early (and welcome) death, the sorry manual worker was promised an eternity

> ... in a vast gulph and lake of Fire ... plunged and rolling in it, all covered and transperced with Fire, which they not only suck in with their Breath, but which enters also at their Eyes and Ears, their Mouths and Nostrils, casting forth dreadful flames, their Skin scorched, their Flesh, Blood, Humours and Brains boiling ...

It was even discovered that, horror of horrors, some *women* were actually degenerate enough to **come their turkeys**. In fact, the very clothes they wore might be a danger; trousers could stimulate the female groin as effectively as a male hand, some authorities believed. It was a pornographer who issued this warning:

> A lady putting on her riding trousers becomes, consciously or unconsciously, akin to a hoyden assuming man's clothes, or nearer still, to a ballet girl drawing on her tights. She is subject to contact of the most perilous kind. The warm close substance that passes close to her flesh, that clasps her loins, and embraces her bum, and insinuates itself between her thighs, has, all senseless leather, cloth or silk, as the case may be, something of the nature of a man's hand in it.

And if it wasn't a woman's clothing that led her astray, it would be that upright length of wickedness, the dildo. In 1672 a bonfire of dildos was made, following the orders of Parliament to destroy French goods. The devices were a mixed batch:

> Some were of wax, where every vein
> And smallest fibre were made plain,
> Some were for tender virgins fit,
> Some for the large salacious slit
> Of a rank lady, tho' so torn
> She hardly feels when a child is born.

The Victorians were especially fond of detailing the dreadful side effects of **wanking** and doing all they could to discourage the practice. A device was invented to control those nocturnal erections that might lead a chap to **clean his rifle**. A metal ring was fastened about the penis and connected to a sinister black box. If the organ expanded beyond a certain size and fitted more snugly in the ring, an electric shock was administered. That delight in punishment was carried over into the slang. Many terms for masturbation involve the idea of beating, flogging, striking and whipping.

Nowadays we know that self-stimulation is healthy, one of the most frequently performed sexual acts and a first-class means of population control, but to name somebody as a pudding-puller is an insult. Oh, it's a weird world, my friends.

Masturbation (or ipsation, as some sexologists have called it) has attracted some interesting technical terms as well as slang ones. Amatripsis describes a woman rubbing or squeezing the labia together, while a man handling himself is manuxorating. Maritate indicates a woman working alone; if she is achieving orgasm by rubbing her thighs together that is syntribation. The term triborgasmia means a wife masturbating her husband.

The practice also has its own anthem; an anonymous music-lover took the cheery 1880 song 'Funiculi Funicula' (composed by one Denza to celebrate the funicular railway in Naples) and added words:

> Last night I stayed up late to masturbate.
> It was so nice! I did it twice!
> Last night I stayed up late to pull my pud.
> It felt so good! I knew it would.
> You should see me working on the short strokes;
> I use my hand. It's simply grand!
> You should see me working on the long strokes.
> I use my feet. It's really neat.
> Smash it! Bash it! Beat it on the floor.
> Smite it! Bite it! Ram it through the door.
> I have some friends who seem to think a fuck is simply grand.
> But for all around enjoyment I prefer it in the hand.

The lyrics were penned about 1960 and the author may have been an American; that is all the information available.

The cultural stuff is done. Here are some alternatives to the W word.

BARCLAY'S. Rhyming slang from the 1930s; in full it is to 'have a Barclay's bank'.

BASHING. A very C19 approach – aggressive and implying punishment.

BAT. A word used in Australia in the first half of the C20. The Aussies are, of course, famous for producing great batsmen.

Bash the Bishop

BEEF. One of the forbidden joys of the C19 was to spend time 'stroking your beef'.

BISHOP, BASH THE, BEAT THE, FLOG THE. Some of the many terms using the image of striking; these are all from the C19 and **bash the bishop** was apparently Army slang. Why a bishop? Because the *glans penis* looks like a chess bishop or a clerical bishop's mitre, according to Eric Partridge.

Determined anti-clericals could go even further and 'murder the bishop'.

BLANKET DRILL. A military exercise that did not appear in the 1930s drill manual but was regularly practised.

BLINDER. This is based on the folklore theory that masturbation makes you go blind.

BOB. A word found in various dialect vocabularies meaning to hit, poke a hole or, appropriately, to toss (as in toss aside).

BONE OFF. Based on a Cockney term for an erection, boner, and used in the early C20.

BOX THE JESUIT AND GET COCKROACHES. This is a long-winded C16 phrase combining a pun on **cock** with the contemporary loathing of the Jesuits who spearheaded the anti-Protestant opposition in England. Box here means to contain rather than fisticuffs.

BRANDLE. A late-C19 literary word meaning to stroke and finger the sex organs; it can be applied to the female or male variety.

BRING OFF, BRING OFF BY HAND. Slang dating back to the C16. The phrases can refer to male and female masturbation.

BRING UP. The expression was often used for any means of inducing sexual desire, not just masturbation.

BUST. Rare C19 slang that has been unobserved for a century and a half.

BUTTER YOUR CORN. The butter in this case is probably semen, as in **buttered bun** (see Chapter 5).

BUTTONHOLE. One of the few terms applying strictly to female masturbation; it was first used in that sense in the C19.

CANDLE BASHING. Like **buttonhole** this is a feminine term, meaning the use of candles by nuns, spinsters, sailors' wives, etc. to satisfy their solitary longings. The C17 poet Sir John Suckling wrote about the candle as dildo; here is part of his effort:

> There is a thing which in the light
> Is seldom used; but in the night
> It serves the female maiden crew,
> The ladies and the good-wives too;
> They use to take it in their hand
> And then it will uprightly stand;
> And to a hole they it apply,
> Where by its goodwill it would die …

CARDINAL. If you had a down on high-ranking priests and lived in the C19, you could spend time 'conking the cardinal' and feel all the better for it.

CHOPSTICKS, PLAYING. Mutual masturbation, a piece of slang from the early C20.

CLAW. This first meant a blow from the cat o' nine tails, but acquired the sexual tint about 1870.

COME YOUR TURKEY. In the 1860s the novel *Nunnery Tales* gave details of the use of a turkey neck filled with assorted materials to create a dildo for young ladies to relieve their urges with.

COOK CUCUMBERS. An image from the 1850s and used only of female masturbation.

CORPORAL AND FOUR, MOUNT A. A rare set of male helpers, who first formed up for duty in the late C18. The mount refers to mounting guard rather than any other activity.

CROWN AND ANCHOR. Rhyming slang for a **wanker**. Crown and anchor is a simple gambling game using dice marked with crowns and, wait for it, anchors.

DAISY. The tender flower could be either pulled or flogged, depending on the gardener's mood.

DIDDLE. One of those Victorian multi-purpose words that meant copulation as well as masturbation.

> There was a young man of Cohoes
> Who diddled himself with his toes,
> He did it so neat
> He betrothed his own feet,
> And christened them Myrtle and Rose

DIGITATE. Fancy-speak for **finger fuck** created by some C19 intellectual tosser.

DISOBEY THE POPE. I am not sure if there has ever been a papal bill specifically prohibiting **coming your turkey**, but the idea of thumbing your nose at the Vatican while **pulling your pudding** may have an appeal to some. Later papal games include 'pleasing the pope' and 'punishing the pope'.

DONKEY, FLOG THE. Another image from the Victorian period, an age obsessed with masturbation and punishment.

DOODLE-DASH. In the C19 a vice indulged in by a **doodle-dasher**. The word pops up in Walter's *My Secret Life* on many occasions, as did, indeed, Walter's doodle.

DRILL FOR OIL. The phrase applies only to female masturbation and was first noted in the 1940s.

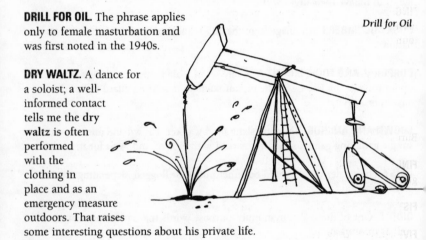

Drill for Oil

DRY WALTZ. A dance for a soloist; a well-informed contact tells me the **dry waltz** is often performed with the clothing in place and as an emergency measure outdoors. That raises some interesting questions about his private life.

DUB. This was popular in the USA around 1910.

DUMMY, FLOG THE. Here dummy stands for a dullard rather than an object a ventriloquist shoves his hand up.

DUTCH HUSBAND, DUTCH WIFE. Cheap to maintain, asks no questions, always willing and doesn't want to talk afterwards – what more could anybody want?

FEEL YOUR WAY TO HEAVEN. A semi-romantic description of vaginal stimulation. At times this is shortened to 'have a feel' or just 'feel'.

FETCH METTLE. Slang going back to the C17, when **mettle** equalled semen. The term has been reduced to 'fetch off' as a variation of fuck off. *Harvard Lampoon* used the instruction in its 1970s parody of Tolkien, *Bored of the Rings*.

FIDDLE. This is an all-purpose word that can refer to the male and female genitals (C19), sexual intercourse (C17) and tossing yourself off (C18).

FINGER, TIP THE LONG FINGER TO. Masturbation or foreplay in the C19.

FINGER FUCK. One of the small number of slang expressions relating to female masturbation; it has been in use since the last part of the C18. Robbie Burns found a home for the term in his bawdy rhymes:

> And ken ye Leezie Lundie, O,
> The godly Leezie Lundie, O,
> She m—s like reek thro' a' the week,
> But f—r f—s on Sunday, O.

Burns (or his printer) inserted the polite dashes in the above verse.

FINGER PIE. A mid-C20 recipe designed to fill a woman with a warm and happy glow.

FIST FUCK. First used in the C19 and still heard today.

FIVE-FINGER MARY. This kind lady has been bringing solace to solitary people since the 1840s.

FIVE-FINGER SHUFFLE. No, not a clever piece of cardsharping, but guess what?

FIVE-FINGERED WIDOW. Like many other merry widows, this one has been around for a long time and knows her stuff.

FLAGPOLE, RUN YOUR HAND UP THE. In the C19 many a patriotic lad hoisted a jack or flag or banner at regular intervals.

FLINGING. A dialect term for manual labour that was heard around 1820.

FLIP YOURSELF OFF. A mid-C20 Australian pastime that could lead over-indulgers to suffer the dire fate of being 'flipwrecked'.

FOUR SISTERS OF THUMB STREET. Good-natured lasses and always ready to lend a helping hand to lonely men. The expression travelled here from America in the late C19.

FREE THE SLAVES. I have no information about the phrase's origin, but it's fun so gets included.

FRIG. A verb with a history in slang back to the 1550s and extracted from the Latin *fricare* (to rub). Though pleasing, the hobby can grow boring, e.g:

> There was a young monk of Siberia,
> Who of frigging grew wearier
> and wearier,
> At last, with a yell,
> He burst from
> his cell,
> And buggered
> the Father
> Superior.

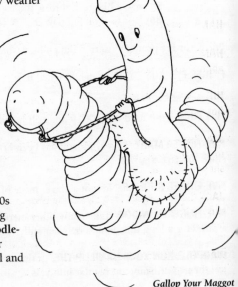

FRIGGLE. A now-forgotten C19 word that sounds like **frig** with a nasty case of baby talk.

GALLOP YOUR MAGGOT. Some Cockney slangmonger of the 1850s created this gem; what a satisfying expression to bellow at some **doodle-dasher** who has irritated you. Far more colourful than the universal and unimaginative 'Wanker!'

Gallop Your Maggot

If you hunger to vary your zoology and exercise a more graceful creature, you can have a go at 'galloping your antelope'.

GERMAN JOB. A name from the early part of the C20, when the rhyming slang for hand was 'German band'.

GET A HANDFUL OF SPRATS. To masturbate a woman; the sprats stand for the salty and fluid aspects of the vagina.

GO BLIND. A late-C19, early-C20 attempt to scare the self-stimulator with the promise of punishment for the misdeed.

HAND GALLOP. The C19 version of a **hand job**, thought up in the days when horses were galloping in all directions.

HAND JOB. A C20 term that describes a basic service in the sex industry; a 'hand gig' is the gay version and a 'hand jig' was available in American gaols in the 1930s.

HAND SHANDY. A term from the first half of the last century.

HANDLE. One of the standard C19 expressions for masturbation, very occasionally applied to women at work.

HOT COCKLES, PLAY. In the C18 the labia were known as the **cockles** so to **play hot cockles** was to masturbate by fondling the labia.

J. ARTHUR. A piece of rhyming slang from the 1940s when J. Arthur Rank seemed to own most of the cinemas in the UK as well as funding the films that were shown in them.

JACK OFF. Originally **jack** meant the penis and intercourse; in the late C19 and early C20 the meaning shifted. In recent years 'Jill off' was created by/for feminists.

JERK OFF. A term from the early C18, short for 'jerk your jelly/juice', this is another example of emigration to the USA being followed by great popularity and success. **Jerk off** is the American **wank/wanker**. In recent years a medical aspect has appeared and people can now 'consult Dr Jerkoff'.

JODRELL BANK. The Cheshire site of the radio telescope of the Nuffield Radio Astronomy Laboratories of Manchester University, opened in the 1950s. Which was when some **wanker** thought up a new piece of rhyming slang for his chosen hobby.

LARK. A simple C19 transfer of meaning from the Standard English word for fun and games.

LING-GRAPPLING. Male stimulation of the female, according to C19 slang, and also sexual intercourse, so a bit of **ling-grappling** could well result in a bit of **ling-grappling**.

LITTLE BROTHER, BEAT YOUR. A phrase used by those who like to imagine the penis as an individual requiring either a name or some other indication of separate identity.

LIZARD. The poor reptile suffered because the complete 1950s phrase is 'whip your lizard'.

LONELY ART. This sounds more like the writer's trade than a solitary pleasure. From the first half of the C20 and containing a good pun on lonely heart.

MADAM PALM AND HER DAUGHTERS. A family enterprise, which opened for business back in the 1840s.

MARY ELLEN. I have no idea who she was, but during the 1940s her handiwork was much appreciated all across the USA. Her associates included Mary Fist, Mary Five-fingers and Mary Palm.

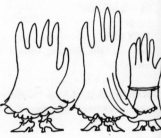

Madam Palm and Her Daughters

MATTRESS FUCKING. Two informants have assured me this was Army slang in the 1930s and 1940s, but I have yet to find a record of it.

MERCHANT BANKER. A financial high-flier who **fiddles** with himself. There is an old riddle that asks: what is the difference between a banker and a **wanker**? Well, a wanker knows what he's doing.

MESS ABOUT. In the C19 and after this indicated groping and heavy petting as well as masturbation. Messing about in boats has long been a hobby with sailors and water rats.

MILK. The word applies to female and male and has been used from the C17 onwards – it turns up early on in a Ben Jonson play. As well as milking yourself, there were a number of unfortunate creatures that could be mistreated; a C19 man might milk the lizard or the moose. (Did you know the moose is so short-sighted that males have been known to hump parked cars? That's what I call servicing a motor.)

MINGO, GO. Masturbation in the 1850s; why mingo is a mystery.

MINNIE FIVE-FINGERS. A descendant of Minnehaha who was busy whooping it up in America in the 1920s.

MISS FIST. For those who prefer sex with an unmarried woman and can't find Miss Laycock or Miss Brown, this lady awaits.

MUTTON. From the C18 onwards mutton jerking and, in the North Country, mutton tugging, have been favourite ways of playing with your food.

ONAN'S OLYMPICS. Which country will collect the most gold medals in this contest?

ONE-LEGGED RACE. An athletic event for a solo runner.

ORGAN SOLO. A non-musical pastime for males on dull afternoons when there's nothing to hand but some curious magazines. Those wanting variety can play a 'lute solo' instead.

PAINT YOUR CEILING. A wild claim about projection and quantity from the 1950s.

PAW-PAW TRICKS. Punning on paw meaning the hand, as well as the fruit, this term from the C19 started out as a nursery warning about bad behaviour: 'No paw-paw tricks!'

PEACOCK, PLAY AT. A poetic usage from the C17 and describing a lady pleasuring herself with a dildo; in Thomas Nashe's ballad about a dildo a happy woman describes hers as

> A knave that moves as light as leaves by wind;
> That bendeth not, nor foldeth any deal;
> But stands as stiff, as he were made of steel,
> And plays at peacock twixt my legs …

PICKLE. More playing with food, as the full expression is 'tickle your pickle'. It later evolved into 'jerkin' the gherkin'.

PINK MATCH, STRIKE THE. A painful-sounding game and not possible with a box of safety matches.

PISSER. For men masturbation is an easy way in which they can 'please their pisser'.

PLAY A SOLO ON THE MEAT FLUTE. A musical pastime from the late 1890s.

PLAY OFF. Not sporting matches, but C18 self-stimulation.

PLAY THE ORGAN. The organ in question is usually male in this slang going back to circa 1910.

PLAY WITH YOURSELF. A C19 expansion of **play off**. The Victorians liked to have things made very clear.

POCKET BILLIARDS, PLAY. An old phrase that has been updated to 'play pocket pool'. As far as I know snooker has yet to become part of the pocket Olympics.

Prune the Fifth Limb

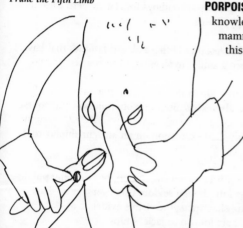

PORPOISE, PUMP YOUR. Even the knowledge that a porpoise is a mammal and not a fish fails to make this sound attractive.

PORK SWORD, PULL THE. A term recorded in the 1960s, but probably older.

PRUNE THE FIFTH LIMB. What a C19 gardener might do in the potting shed, if he couldn't tempt anyone in to help him sift loam.

PUDDING, PULL YOUR. Another example of the fun to be had toying with your meals. This is C19 slang but is still in use. Minor variations of the phrase are 'pull your pud' and 'play with your pudden'.

PULL ABOUT. Partridge considers this to be a vulgar phrase rather than slang; whichever you pick, the expression was conjured up in the C19.

Pull Your Pudding

PULL OFF. Always used by males, generally in the phrase 'pull yourself off'. First noted in the mid-C19.

PUMP OFF. PE for the wrist in late-Victorian and early-Edwardian times.

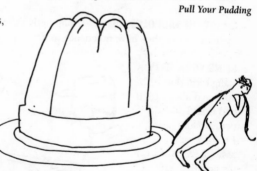

RIFLE, CLEAN YOUR. This command is not found in the standard-issue drill manual, and any private tinkering with his privates may find that the sergeant major is out to make him suffer.

ROLL YOUR OWN MARBLES. A pastime for schoolboys for several centuries; it is likely to continue to fill many happy hours.

ROSY PALM AND HER FIVE SISTERS. Another of those all-girl families that have done so much since the C19 to bring smiles to faces.

RUB UP. Foreplay as well as masturbation in this long-standing term; it has been around since about 1650. **Rub off** also exists, but more often means intercourse.

SAILOR'S JOY. A late-C19 and early-C20 expression for an ancient shipboard occupation.

SHAG. For most of the world this word now means coition, but in many public schools **shag** means a **wank**. (The full, though seldom used, version is 'shag your hand'.) Acne and pimples are shag spots, the visible evidence of over-indulgence; in America these are known as jack bumps.

SHAKE. A slice of slang that was in active service from 1550 to the early C19. It was replaced by the more detailed instruction: shake up.

SHAKE HANDS WITH THE WIFE'S BEST FRIEND. Not the milkman, but the husband's wedding tackle; in his view, the best thing that's happened to his partner.

SHOOT THE TADPOLES. Sperm are popularly called tadpoles and their evacuation by hand means they have no chance to develop into sprogs.

Shoot the Tadpoles

SLING YOUR JELLY. A slang term that appeared about 1870 and is still occasionally heard, I have been assured. A version that has disappeared was 'sling your juice'.

SOLDIER'S JOY. This gave pleasure to slangsters from 1850–1910. In the Royal Navy, it should be noted, the phrase is a name for pease pudding, a wholesome and nourishing dish that provides much-needed energy.

SPLASH. Messy masturbation carried out in the 1930s.

STINK-FINGER. Male masturbation of a female described in a slang term dating back to circa 1840. It often appears as 'play at stink-finger'. Walter writes:

> I have fucked something like twelve hundred women, and have
> felt the cunts of three hundred others of whom I have seen one
> hundred and fifty naked. My acquaintance with the others
> beginning and ending mostly in the streets, with the delicate
> operation of what is called stink-fingering.

STIR, STIR IT UP. Slang from the 1940s and 1950s describing work carried out by women only.

STIR YOUR STEW. What all good cooks were up to in the mid-C20.

SWEEP YOUR OWN CHIMNEY. DIY clearing of the flues from the end of the C19.

SWORD, POLISH YOUR. The pastime of bold knights on wet, winter nights and another slice of energetic, martial slang from the C19.

TICKLE YOUR CRACK. A C19 expression that applied specifically to women.

TIT-WANK. Using a woman's breasts instead of getting manual stimulation. In highfalutin words this is *coitus a mammilla*. Also known as a titty fuck and Dutch fuck in recent decades.

TONK. From 1910 this name was applied to a great Australian hobby.

TOSS. First recorded in 1780 and usually in the form 'toss off', this verb has lasted and lasted; it is widely used today, second only to **wank**, though **jerk off** is gaining ground.

TOUCH UP. Like **rub up** this began by meaning foreplay (in the 1760s) then later took on the meaning of intercourse and by the 1890s meant masturbation. These days it seems to have reverted to its first meaning.

TUG, GIVE A. A sample of slang handiwork that has been around since the early 1920s; I heard it used in a Cambridge pub in 2003. An Australian variation is to 'have a tug'; this was in use in the 1950s.

UNCLOG YOUR PIPES. This sounds more like DIY plumbing than having fun.

WANK. The main term for self-stimulation, though heard as abuse as often as (more often than?) a sexual description. Originally spelled whank, it arrived in 1870 or so without much history and has steadily replaced older slang. The word is probably linked to the dialect verb whang, meaning to beat or strike.

WANKER. Slang in some minor public schools for a bloater, kipper or other smoked fish.

WIDOW HAND. Another helpful lady from the C19.

WIRE, PULL YOUR. Which particular wire is not specified in this C19 instruction.

WORK YOURSELF OFF. Partridge's dictionary dates this expression back to the C16 and says it was old even then.

7. GROPING FOR TROUTS

Many years ago somebody said to me, 'There's no need to use four-letter words in your stories; Shakespeare never did.' Oh no? What about **cock, tool, yard, hole, hook** and **ring**, all used in a sexual sense by the Master of Masters. What the speaker meant was that Shakespeare (like John Cleland in *Fanny Hill*) did not use **fuck** or **cunt**, though Shakespeare punned on **country** and made a joke of almost spelling out the word in *Twelfth Night*. The steward Malvolio sees a letter penned by his employer, Countess Olivia, and exclaims: 'By my life, this is my lady's hand! These be her very C's, her U's and her T's; and thus she makes her great P's.'

Shakespeare liked to joke and pun; he loved finding new ways of describing old acts and organs. Not that he ignored the slang of the day; **dart, needle, potato finger, sword, weapon, prick, crack, Venus's glove** and **dormouse** appear in his works. The ability to blend old and new, high and low language, and view sex as just another part of everyday life as well as an elemental force help make Shakespeare great.

The terms listed represent only a fraction of the bawdy and randy language Shakespeare used. We cannot say if he invented them all but often he was the first (or only) author to commit them to print. Always remember, Shakespeare's plays are like sex: the more you know, the more fun you have.

ACT OF SHAME, ACT OF SPORT. Sexual intercourse, according to speeches in *Othello* and *Troilus and Cressida,* offering contrasting points of view on the same event.

ACTION. Copulation in *Pericles*; men were demanding a piece of the action long before the 1960s.

ACTIVITY. This means male sexual power and confidence, which could be sapped by a woman, as Pandarus warns in *Troilus and Cressida*: 'She'll bereave you o' th'deeds too, if she calls your activity in question.'

AFFAIRS. The vagina is called this in Sonnet 151: 'He is contented thy poor drudge to be, To stand in thy affairs.'

AMOROUSLY IMPLEACHT. This poetic phrase, in which impleacht means interwoven, indicates a penis surrounded by the vagina's hair.

ANOTHER THING. The sex organs, female and male, according to remarks in *King Lear, Henry IV Part 1, Henry VIII* and *Two Gentlemen of Verona*. In *Lear* the words about the penis are sinister: 'She that's a maid now ... shall not be a maid long, unless things be cut shorter.' Ouch.

ASS. Shakespeare's pun on arse and a man riding on his ass is found in *Love's Labour's Lost*.

AUNT. A whore or promiscuous woman; when the thief Autolycus in *The Winter's Tale* sings about tumbling in the hay with his aunts he is not displaying a perverse taste for his blood relatives.

BACK, HAVE A HOT. To be randy, according to *The Merry Wives of Windsor*. A forerunner of 'hot to trot' and 'she was hot for it'.

BAG AND BAGGAGE. In *The Winter's Tale* the bag is the scrotum and the baggage is the penis. See **Let in, let out.**

BALDRICK. See **Hang your bugle on an invisible baldrick.**

BANKRUPT BEGGAR. A man who is exhausted by sex (*The Rape of Lucrece*). The penis is the beggar whose fortune (semen) has all drained away.

BASIMECU. 'Monsieur Basimecu, the dauphin of France' is an insult, **Basimecu** being a phonetic spelling of *baise mon cul*, meaning kiss my arse.

BAUBLE. In *Romeo and Juliet* the word means the penis, which is connected to a fool who 'runs lolling up and down to hide his bauble in a hole'.

BAWDRY. Shacking up or living together without the benefit of wedlock. In *As You Like It* there is the proposal: 'Come, sweet Audrey; we must be married or live in bawdry.'

BAWL. The testicles, featuring in *Henry IV Part 2*.

BEAGLE. A whore in *Timon of Athens* but simply an ordinary young woman in *Twelfth Night*.

BEAST WITH TWO BACKS, MAKE THE. A famous description of a copulating couple resembling some creature with two heads, two backs and eight assorted limbs. The words are from *Othello*, Act 1, where Iago tells Brabantio: 'Your daughter and the Moor are now making the beast with two backs.'

BED-PRESSER. Somebody who spends much time between the sheets and not sleeping; Prince Hal calls Falstaff 'this bed-presser' and it is not a compliment.

BED-RITE. Copulation viewed as something more than a pleasure, but a legal and social obligation the couple must acknowledge.

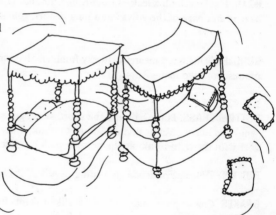

Bed-swerver

BED-SWERVER. Someone who regularly cheats on a spouse. Unfairly this is used of women rather than men; in *The Winter's Tale* Leontes refers to his wife Hermione by the term.

BEG A CHILD OF. 'I think he means to beg a child of her' (*Henry VI Part 3*) means he is planning to ask the woman to sleep with him.

BEHIND-DOOR WORK. Casual sex, usually between servants, groundlings and minor characters.

BELLY. At different times Shakespeare uses the word for the vagina, the womb and the stomach and groin.

BILLIARDS. Used as a joking reference to balls (as contained in the scrotum).

BIRD'S NEST. The female sex organ and pubic hair. In *Romeo and Juliet* the old Nurse tells Juliet she will 'fetch a ladder, By the which your love must climb a bird's nest soon when it is dark.'

BLACKNESS. The vagina as named by Iago in *Othello*.

BOARD A LAND CARACK. Sexual intercourse, probably paid for by the man. A carack or carrack was a big merchant ship and worth boarding for plunder.

BOAT. 'Her boat hath a leak' is from *King Lear* and implies the woman has VD. Boat as an image of the vulva has a long history, going back to Roman times (see Chapter 8).

BOGGLER. This word means a clumsy fumbler. Shakespeare employs it for a promiscuous woman – Antony refers to Cleopatra as 'a boggler ever' when he's having a hissy fit.

BOTTOM GRASS. Pubic hair and the short, sweet grass of meadows. In the poem *Venus and Adonis*, Venus invites Adonis to think of her as a park and himself as a deer with the right to nibble the best the park can offer.

BOX UNSEEN. The pudenda, according to *All's Well That Ends Well*.

BRAKES. Coarse pubic hair, unlike the silken skeins found at **bottom grass**.

BREAK THE PALE. The pale is the fence round a deer park and sometimes a sneaky stag 'breaks the pale, And feeds from home,' according to *The Comedy of Errors*.

BROACH. When a cask or barrel is broached, it is opened and used. Now apply the image to a woman, as Shakespeare did in *Antony and Cleopatra*.

BULLETS. A double meaning to this code; the **bullets** are the balls and semen. When, in *Henry IV Part 1*, the Hostess tells Falstaff and Pistol, 'I'll drink no proofs nor bullets,' it's clear she doesn't swallow.

BUM. The old and trusted slang for buttocks, appearing in *Measure for Measure* ('Your bum is the greatest thing about you') and in *A Midsummer Night's Dream* in the following pratfall described by Puck:

> The wisest aunt, telling the saddest tale,
> Sometimes for three-foot stool mistaketh me;
> Then I slip from her bum and down topples she.

Think of that the next time somebody tells you the elderly were treated with more respect in the past.

BUNG. The anus, though some authorities believe Shakespeare used bung as short for bung-nipper, a cutpurse or thief.

BURDEN. This describes the weight of a man pressing down on a woman during sex.

BURIED WITH HER FACE UP. The correct interment position for a woman who has died of an excess of love, according to *Much Ado About Nothing*. The modern equivalent would be 'buried in a Y-shaped coffin'.

Bum

BUSINESS. Copulation and other sexual activities in *Antony and Cleopatra*. Modern-day prostitutes use the word.

BUTT. Short for the buttocks and used as an oath, e.g. 'you ruinous butt, you whoreson indistinguishable cur' (*Troilus and Cressida*). However, certain scholars claim the sense of the word is that of a large barrel.

BUZ, BUZZ. Not the sound of busy bees on a summer afternoon but the Elizabethan stage convention for imitating a fart. When Hamlet says 'Buz, buz!' to Polonius he's actually blowing a couple of raspberries in the old chap's face.

CALL TO A RECKONING. Ordering a woman for pleasure and having her put on the bill – the **reckoning**. This is still possible in some hotels; the lady appears as 'extra bedclothes' on the bill. Bed linen, if the hotel is upmarket.

CARNAL STRINGS. The control lines that lust and love tug on to operate humans. Iago talks to Othello of 'Our raging motions, our carnal strings, our unbitted lusts'. That 'unbitted' refers to a horse not having a bridle and bit fitted to give the rider control.

CARROT. The penis as a root vegetable.

Catastrophe

WHAT A
CATASTROPHE!

CATASTROPHE. When Falstaff threatens to 'tickle your catastrophe', watch out, because he's not planning to make you laugh. This is another pun on **ass** (arse) – the 'as' in **catastrophe**.

CHANGE THE COD'S HEAD FOR THE SALMON'S TAIL. This is where it gets poetic and complicated. The **cod's head** is the penis (think of codpiece) and the **salmon's tail** is the vagina. OK? Now, **change** here means to put in. Get the picture? The words are from *Othello* and indicate copulation in a fancy fashion (the indication, that is, not the copulation).

CHARGED CHAMBER. An elaborate image from siege warfare to describe the testicles. Castles would have mines sunk beneath them by the attacking forces; chambers at the ends of the tunnels would be packed with combustibles and set alight. The fire would weaken the wall and cause its collapse. Shakespeare is comparing the testicles with the loaded chamber waiting to burst into action.

The speech containing the **charged chamber** also mentions a breach (meaning vagina) and a **pike** (penis) and you can read it for yourself in *Henry IV Part 2*.

CHASTE TREASURE. Virginity locked away in a safe secured by the hymen.

CIRCLE. The vagina is called thus in *Romeo and Juliet*.

CITY. A woman's view of her maidenhead as a city subject to siege by men; in *A Lover's Complaint* the lady says, 'Long upon these terms I held my city, Till thus he 'gan besiege me.'

CLACK DISH. The plate a beggar uses to collect money in (nowadays usually a clack cap). The dish was rattled to attract the attention of generous folk – think of the Sally Army lasses shaking their cans. In the play *Measure for Measure* the **clack dish** is the **cunt**, also being waggled to raise money.

CLEAVE THE PIN. Making a man ejaculate, as used in *Love's Labour's Lost*: 'Then she will get the upshot by cleaving the pin.' The method used is not indicated.

CLIFF. A female breast, perhaps a specific one of a swarthy shade because Shakespeare wrote, 'If snow be white, why then her breasts are dun' (from Sonnet 130) and in *The Comedy of Errors* a character says, 'Where England? I looked for the chalky cliffs, but I could find no whiteness in them.'

COCK. Still a favourite word for the penis and one to flash at those silly souls who still believe Shakespeare did not use 'crude' words. Quote Pistol's boast that 'Pistol's cock is up, And flashing fire will follow' from *Henry V* at such prudes. (See **bullets**.)

COIN. This is Shakespeare drawing on technology for fun; a man **coins** children as a mint coins money. The father of a child is the coiner and if some other man has slipped into the marriage bed and done the deed, the bastard child is thus a counterfeit. The image appears in the play *Cymbeline*: 'some coiner with his tools, Made me a counterfeit'.

COLT. Intercourse in *Cymbeline*, where Posthumus says, 'She hath been colted by him.' Randy stallions are said to be feeling coltish; any rider who has tried to handle a coltish stallion knows how hard it is.

COME. Exactly what it means today: to reach orgasm and ejaculate. Found in various of the plays.

COME INTO MY CHAMBER. A woman's invitation to her lover, for example. Cressida to Troilus: 'My lord, come you again into my chamber.' And that's after a night of passion.

COME OVER. Another expression for intercourse, found in *Much Ado About Nothing*.

COMPOUND. Coition is so described in *King Lear*, where sex and astrology mingle: 'My father compounded with my mother under the dragon's tail and my nativity was under ursa major; so that it follows, I am rough and lecherous.'
    NB: the dragon's tail is an astrological term here and not the latter end of a mythological beast.

CONGER. A large (and savage) eel with a streamlined shape that calls to mind the penis.

CONJURE IT DOWN. A woman's magical power can make an erection vanish – by giving the man an orgasm. The trick is mentioned in *Romeo and Juliet*.

CORNER. The vagina, and perhaps a name reduced from the French *petit coin*. Othello says this about Desdemona in one of his jealous furies: 'I'd rather be a toad than keep a corner in the thing I love/For others' uses.' (See **corner cupboard** in Chapter 2.)

COUNTRY, COUNTRY MATTERS. Somewhat obvious puns on **cunt**, the most famous example being Hamlet asking Ophelia, 'Do you think I meant country matters?'

CRACK. This is both the vagina and defloration; in *Pericles* the order is given, 'take her away; use her at thy pleasure; crack the glass of her virginity'.

DANCE WITH YOUR HEELS. Shakespeare is describing a woman's heels bouncing on the bed during sex.

DEAREST BODILY PART. The pudendum is called this in *Cymbeline*, when Iachimo boasts, 'I have enjoyed the dearest bodily part of your mistress' – a thing no gentleman would do, of course.

DEMESNES. When a woman's body is thought of as a **park**, the **demesnes** are her lap, vulva and buttocks. The image is from *Romeo and Juliet*.

Dance with Your Heels

DIAL. At different times both a clock's dial and a sundial are used to mean the female sex organ. The gnomon – the sundial's shadow-tossing pin – stands for the male organ.

DIE, DIE IN A WOMAN'S LAP. Orgasm; King Lear claims he 'will die bravely like a smug bridegroom'.

DISEDGE. To blunt the sharp edge of a sexual appetite; it generally refers to a woman **grinding** down a man.

DISH. The word indicates the same thing as recent slang: a lovely woman. 'A woman is a dish for the gods, if the devil dress her not' (*Antony and Cleopatra*).

DISHEARTEN. Another word for leaving a fellow shagged out.

DIVER. The man seen as a plunger into the lake of the vagina.

DO. Coition, as in *Titus Andronicus*: 'I have done thy mother.'

DRAW. Displaying the penis, based on a man drawing a sword from its scabbard. Hence this dialogue from *Romeo and Juliet*:

> Gregory: Draw thy tool, here comes two of the house
> of the Montagues.
> Sampson: My naked weapon is out.

Of course, 'tool' here meant a sword. Of course.

DRIBBLING DART OF LOVE. Is there anybody out there who doesn't get this one? Is there any male who hasn't experienced this?

ERINGO, ERYNGO. The root of the sea holly and considered an aphrodisiac. The white root could grow up to seven feet long; it was sliced up, candied and sold to those with flagging energies and appetites. Shakespeare mentions it in *The Merry Wives of Windsor*.

ET CETERA. The literal meaning of the Latin is 'and other things' and the other thing in Shakespeare's mind was the vagina. 'O that she were An open et-cetera' is in *Romeo and Juliet*. The American poet e e cummings wrote about lying in the mud of the First World War trenches:

> (dreaming,
> et
> cetera, of
> Your smile
> eyes knees and of your Etcetera)

Which shows that poets never allow a useful image to fade away.

EXCHANGE FLESH. To have intercourse, usually said of a woman, as in these words from *The Winter's Tale*: 'It is thought she was a woman, and was turn'd into a cold fish for she would not exchange flesh with one that loved her.'

FAIR PARTS. The penis and scrotum are indicated by this phrase.

FEED FROM HOME. The Shakespearean equivalent of the modern idea of playing away from home.

FERE. A friend or companion, though a mistress is usually described by this term: 'The king took unto him a fere, Who died and left a female heir' (*Pericles*).

FLESH YOUR WILL ON. Sexual action from the male point of view: 'He hath perverted a young gentlewoman ... and this night he fleshes his will.' This almost certainly is based on the idea of 'fleshing your sword', i.e. wounding or killing an opponent.

FOIN. Fucking. Falstaff is asked by his light o' love Doll Tearsheet, 'When wilt thou leave fighting o' days and foining o' nights?'

FORFENDED PLACE. The female groin as a forbidden and defended zone.

FOUNTAIN. The female breasts, according to Venus who invites her lover to 'Stray lower, where the pleasant fountains lie,' in the poem *Venus and Adonis*.

FOUTRE. Used as an oath: 'A foutre for thine office.' Foutre is French for intercourse. Geddit?

Fountain

FRENCH VELVET. The full phrase is 'piled for French velvet' and it means somebody has a bad case of VD, Cupid's measles, pox, call it what you will.

GERMEN. In a medical sense this is an ovary but old Bill applies the noun to semen.

GETTING UP. Intercourse followed by pregnancy and used in *The Merchant of Venice*.

GO TO IT. Fornication. King Lear denounces 'a simpering dame that minces virtue' who will 'go to it with a more riotous appetite' than a coltish stallion.

GREASY, GREASILY. To talk dirty, according to *Love's Labour's Lost*: 'Come, come, you talk greasily; your lips grow foul.' Falstaff, that tun of lard and lechery, is referred to as 'This greasy knight'.

GROPING FOR TROUTS IN A PECULIAR RIVER. Fishing into somebody else's private stream or having a woman you should not have. A great expression for adultery and found in this exchange in *Measure for Measure*:

> Pompey: Yonder man is carried to prison.
> Mistress Overdone: What has he done?
> Pompey: A woman.
> Mistress Overdone: But what's his offence?
> Pompey: Groping for trouts in a peculiar river.

HANG YOUR BUGLE ON AN INVISIBLE BALDRICK. Benedick in *Much Ado About Nothing* plans to do this with his bugle (horn): the phrase means sexual intercourse. And Benedick (good dick) should be hot stuff.

HICK AND HACK. A Shakespearean way of saying skirt-chasing and humping.

Hobby Horse

HILLOCK. This is Venus again advertising her attractions to Adonis with talk of her 'Round rising hillocks', or bum.

HIT, HIT IT. Sex, on the same lines as verbs like **knock** and bang.

HOBBY HORSE. This means a rocking horse and a mistress who moves like one during sex. The expression appears in the two great jealousy plays: *The Winter's Tale* and *Othello*.

HOLY-THISTLE. A prick that goes into a hole – a topic raised in a conversation in *Much Ado*.

IT. Copulation. The word has stayed with English speakers until the present day.

JUGGLE, JUGGLING. Getting your end away, in modern terms, or perhaps playing with your balls in public for money. I mean busking, of course. A juggler was a randy nuisance; Doll Tearsheet calls Pistol 'you basket-hilt stale juggler'.

JUMP. A dialect term for sex that is still heard in the North Country. *The Winter's Tale* contains the advice: 'Jump her and thump her.' It implies a vigorous performance by the man involved.

KATE. Along with Moll and Doll this was a conventional name for a prostitute and used by Shakespeare in *Measure for Measure*.

KNOT. The intertwining arms and legs of lovers are meant by this **knot**, not your granny, reef or sheepshank. And not always tied in a pleasant environment, according to *Othello*: 'A cistern for foul toads/To knot and gender in'.

LADY-BIRD. A woman with very loose morals and considerable popularity.

LAY DOWN. To persuade a woman to get into position for sex; in *Henry VIII* Englishmen who have lived in France are said to have mastered 'a speeding trick to lay down ladies', which was not approved of by stay-at-home types.

LAY IT TO YOUR HEART. In *Much Ado About Nothing* the words indicate a woman welcoming a man to her body.

LET IN, LET OUT. This describes the act of sexual intercourse; in *The Winter's Tale* the jealous king Leontes thinks his wife is unfaithful and that lust will 'let in and let out the enemy with bag and baggage'. (See **bag and baggage**.)

LIE ON. A basic description of copulation found in *Othello*:

> Iago: Lie –
> Othello: With her?
> Iago: With her, on her, what you will.

Shakespeare also uses 'lie on her back' for a specifically female point of view.

LINE, LINED. A word for coition found in *As You Like It* (a suggestive title, what?): 'Winter garments must be lined./So must slender Rosalind.' The Rosalind I tried the suggestion on was certainly slender but owned a vicious left hook that featured in her reply.

MAKE A MONSTER OF A MAN. To make a man a cuckold, a fate threatened in this way in *King John* and *Hamlet*.

MAMMETS. A woman's breasts are called **mammets** by the all-action Hotspur in *Henry IV Part 1*: 'I care not for thee, Kate; this is no world to play with mammets and to tilt with lips.'

MANSION OF LOVE. The body as a pleasure ground for love rather than a temple. There is a cruel aspect to the image, as well; a victim in *The Rape of Lucrece* is said to have 'Her mansion battered by the enemy'.

MARROW. Semen, also called **mettle**. *Timon of Athens* offers this comment on the young: 'Lust and liberty,/Creep in the minds and marrows of our youth that against the stream of virtue they may strive.'

MELT. An orgasm, used for both sexes enjoying the experience.

MINGLE BLOODS. An expression for copulation found in *The Winter's Tale*.

MISTRESS KATE KEEPDOWN. A whore, Kate being a name often given to trulls, and a good one, who kept men down on the bed.

MOMENTARY TRICK. Sexual intercourse, short-lasting if the man is in too much of a hurry, and with all the unpleasant consequences that brief pleasure brings.

MORT O' THE DEER. In hunting the **mort** is the death of the deer; the little death your dear undergoes is the orgasm. 'To be paddling palms and pinching fingers

... then to sigh, as 'twere /The mort o' the deer,/ O that is entertainment my bosom likes not.' A complaint from a jealous man in *The Winter's Tale*.

NAKED SEEING SELF. The vulva is called this in *Henry V*.

NEST OF SPICERY. The vagina and pubic hair, according to Richard III, who thought of his niece's body in this way.

O. The female sex organ as a magic **circle**, not to mention a sound of surprise: 'Perchance he like a full-acorn'd boar, Cried "O!" and mounted,' it says in *Cymbeline*.

OCCUPY. To copulate and, according to *Henry IV Part 2*, a word 'which was an excellent good word before it was ill sorted'.

Mort o' the Deer

OFFEND IN A DREAM. A wet dream, whose content might include enjoying all sorts of people one couldn't pleasure in waking life.

OLD LING. A woman reduced to her sexual organ, the equivalent of calling her a cunt today.

PACE. To train a woman for sexual purposes; Shakespeare's version of what is now called grooming.

PADDLE. There is something particularly lascivious and warm about this word – which simply means stroking and caressing with the palm of the hand. It suggests secrecy and the spice of sin. You can find it in *Hamlet*, *The Winter's Tale* and *Othello*.

PARK. The female body considered as a pleasure ground reserved for a particular man's use. Poachers and trespassers were to be prosecuted or, far better, flogged.

As a youth Shakespeare is alleged to have poached Sir Thomas Lucy's deer; nothing is mentioned about any interaction with Lady Lucy.

PECULIAR RIVER. (See Groping for trouts …)

PIKE. The penis regarded as a twelve-foot-long weapon of war, particularly effective against cavalry.

PILLICOCK, PILLICOCK-HILL. In *King Lear* Edgar, posing as a wandering madman, sings 'Pillicock sat on Pillicock hill,/Halloo, halloo, loo, loo!' It has been assumed that the words indicated the **tool** and **quim**. The scholar Eric Partridge, however, believes that **pillicock** means the penis and testicles, while **pillicock-hill** is the Mount of Venus.

PISS YOUR TALLOW. Something that joggers and gym-haunters do regularly: shed weight by sweating gallons. It was also used to mean ejaculation.

PLAY ON YOUR BACK. A woman's part in the sex act, i.e. lie back and enjoy it. Used by the Bard in *Titus Andronicus*.

PLUM. The female sex organs, owing to their external shape and their having a groove like certain varieties of plum.

POLL-AXE. Yet again the fantasy of the penis as a dangerous weapon; in *Love's Labour's Lost* we hear of 'Your lion, that holds his poll-axe sitting on a close-stool' Here 'lion' means a conceited man and a 'close-stool' is a chamber-pot.

POTENT REGIMENT. The full wedding tackle sported by a man; Antony parades his **potent regiment** for Cleopatra rather than his wife.

PRINT OFF. The printing trade is the source of this image, which means a woman has produced a child who looks like her husband: 'Your mother was most true to wedlock, prince;/For she did print your royal father off, conceiving you' (*The Winter's Tale*).

PROMPTURE OF THE BLOOD. A craving for sexual relations with a particular person, ranging from a one-night stand to a long-term arrangement.

PUNK. A whore, described by a shortening of the Latin word *punctum*, meaning a small hole, one made by a little prick.

PUT A MAN IN YOUR BELLY. Celia speaks of sexual intercourse in this way in *As You Like It*.

PUT DOWN. Not something the vet will do to a leaky old dog, but to lay a lady down for sex. There is a hint of force about the expression.

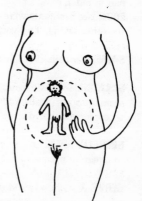

PUZZEL. A trollop, trull, **punk** or plain prostitute. 'Puccelle or puzzel, dolphin or dogfish,/Your hearts I'll stamp out with my horse's heels' (*Henry VI Part 1*). The word is taken from the nickname of Joan of Arc, *La Pucelle de France* (the Virgin of France) who was warmly disliked by the English.

Put a Man in Your Belly

QUAIL. In *Troilus and Cressida* a character is described as 'An honest fellow enough, and one that loves quail', meaning he was a lad for the birds. The **quail** was young and had loose knicker-elastic. In the USA 'San Quentin quail' were the jailbait that landed you in San Quentin Prison.

RAVEN. No, not a large black bird with a hoarse voice and lodgings in the Tower of London, but a verb meaning to enjoy rough-trade fornication.

RESPECT. What so many people are looking for, it seems. In *Measure for Measure* it equals intercourse: 'I respected with her before I married to her,' boasts Pompey. The old question, 'Will you respect me in the morning?' takes on a fresh meaning.

RIGGISH. Randy, lecherous, lascivious, gagging for it. A disapproving Roman says of Cleopatra: 'Vilest things become themselves in her … the holy priests bless her when she is riggish.'

ROGER. In Shakespeare's day a name often given to a dog and the penis.

RUDDER. A term for the bottom and the vagina that appears in *Antony and Cleopatra*: 'My heart was tied to thy rudder by strings ...' Curious habits they had in olden days. I heard the word used in a local supermarket in summer 2004; two assistants were unloading goods in a narrow aisle and one pushed by the other saying, 'Pull your rudder in, mate.'

SALMON'S TAIL. (See **Change the cod's head ...**)

SCRATCH. To masturbate, especially a man caressing a woman. In *The Tempest* a seaman's song recalls Kate, who hated sailors, but 'a tailor might scratch her wherever she itched'.

SECRETLY OPEN. Of a woman, to be sexually open (physically and emotionally) to a man in private.

SERVE. A stallion is said to serve a mare and the process can be exhausting for all concerned. Our Bill noted as much in *Henry IV Part 2*: 'To serve bravely is to come halting off, you know.' Here halting means limping or lame.

SHAKE A MAN'S BACK. A woman can test a man's skill and stamina by bucking and plunging in bed, as Henry V knew well: 'Methought yesterday your mistress shrewdly shook your back.' The image comes from horsemanship.

SING. A woman who sings is one making advances to a man and then having sex with him.

SINK IN. What a man intends to do with his penis – sink in and stay in. A dainty morsel from *Romeo and Juliet*.

SLUICE. A satisfyingly sloshy and liquid word for intercourse, found in *The Winter's Tale*; as usual it is a jealous husband speaking:

> Many a man there is holds his wife by th'arm
> That little thinks she has been sluiced in his absence
> And his pond fished by his next neighbour, by Sir
> Smile, his neighbour.

SOLDIER, BE A GOOD SOLDIER TO A LADY. The man who is skilled in flirting, seduction and screwing is a **good soldier** in the eyes of a woman with the experience to recognise his talents. The phrase appears in *Much Ado About Nothing*.

SPEND. A word that was still widely used in the C19, meaning to have an orgasm and discharge. In *All's Well That Ends Well* a young man is accused of 'Spending his manly marrow' in his mistress's arms.

SPIN OFF. Another manufacturing metaphor, this time from spinning flax to make linen, and meaning to make a man ejaculate.

SPIT WHITE. Falstaff's description of ejaculation.

STAB. Coition as knife-play in *Henry IV Part 2* where the Hostess of the sordid tavern complains: 'He stabbed me in mine own house and that most beastly; in good faith, he cares not what mischief he doth, if his weapon be out; he will foin like any devil.' (See also **foin**.)

STAIR-WORK. Like **trunk work** this was casual sex in any dark corner that offered temporary refuge for the lovers.

STAMP. Shakespeare again drawing on the industrial revolution of his day for a way of describing the making of children; here the child is a product of the die-stamping process.

STANDARD. The penis viewed as a tall shaft with a banner on top.

STEAL A SHIVE OF A CUT LOAF. To have sex with a married woman, the Shakespearean version of 'Nobody misses one more slice off a cut cake'. The phrase is found in *Titus Andronicus*.

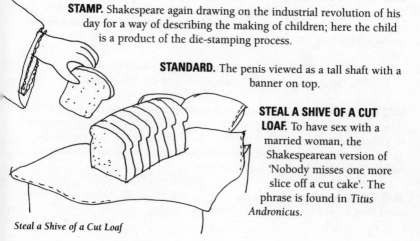
Steal a Shive of a Cut Loaf

STRIKE. Intercourse as aggression in this word appearing in *Titus Andronicus*, where it describes the gang-rape of Lavinia:

> ... strike, brave boys, and take your turns;
> There serve your lust, shadow'd from Heaven's eyes
> And revel in Lavinia's treasury.

STRIVE. Sexual wrestling, the emphasis being on foreplay and sport rather than violation.

STUMBLE. To persuade a woman to have sex, with a suggestion of her being more than willing to trip.

SUNBURNT. 'The Grecian dames are sunburnt, and not worth the splinter of a lance' (*Troilus and Cressida*) does not mean the ladies had spent too long on the beach but that they were burnt with VD. The lance is the penis, of course, and you can guess what splintering it means.

SUPPLY THE PLACE. Shakespeare means taking a husband's place in the family four-poster; he used the image in *King Lear*.

SWORDS AND BUCKLERS. Penises and vaginas. **Sword** was an established description of the penis; a **buckler** is a large shield with an ornamental boss, which some writers think resembles the Mount of Venus. Shakespeare wrote this in *Much Ado About Nothing*:

> Benedick: Call Beatrice: I give thee the bucklers.
> Margaret: Give us the swords; we have bucklers of our own.

TAKE IT. The phrase indicates both a willingness to be seduced and the physical act of taking the penis into the vagina. It forms a piece of political advice given to Richard (about to be the III) by the Duke of Buckingham: 'Play the maid's part – still answer nay, and take it.' Buckingham is talking about the crown being offered to Richard.

TAKE OFF. Reducing a man's sexual power by copulation; Hamlet tells Ophelia she'd have to do a lot of groaning to take off his edge.

THING. This is the vagina when Falstaff is joking with the Hostess in *Henry IV Part 1*:

> Falstaff: Go, you thing, go.
> Hostess: Say, what thing? What thing?
> Falstaff: What thing! Why, a thing to thank God on.

Magically, when Anne Bullen talks to Lord Sands in *Henry VIII*, the **thing** becomes the penis. **Another thing** is a variant found in *The Two Gentlemen of Verona*.

THREE-INCH FOOL. A man with a small penis is described this way in *The Taming of the Shrew*.

TIRE ON. Another of those terms for describing the shagged-out male.

TOP. Copulation at its most basic. Iago says to Othello: 'Would you, the supervisor, grossly gape on and behold her topped?' It may be a variation of the word **tup**.

TOWN BULL. Shorthand for the randy, rapacious male who is convinced that every woman he encounters is longing for his attentions.

TOY. To have sexual fun – kissing, fondling, tickling, etc. as well as intercourse. Passionate but playful, the scholar Eric Partridge suggests.

TRIP. Applied to a woman, it means giving in to a man's sexual demands; in *Troilus and Cressida* the Trojan men are said to be good at tripping up young women.

TRUNK WORK. A pun on the idea of having sex in large clothes trunks and the action of two human trunks working away in coition.

TUP. Shakespeare giving us a hint of his days in rural Warwickshire – **tup** is the technical word

Tup

for the mating of sheep. *Othello* provides a famous quote: 'Even now, now, very now, an old black ram is tupping your white ewe.' That's Iago commenting on the wedding night of Desdemona and Othello.

UNION. The sexual act, uniting the couple in their single existence. From *The Tempest*: 'The union of your bed.'

USE. When employed in *Romeo and Juliet* by the Nurse, the word means sexual pleasure in general – she says Juliet will be no use without Romeo. In *Titus Andronicus* **use** denotes intercourse: 'Did you not use his daughter very friendly?'

VELVET LEAVES. The **velvet** is the clitoris and the **leaves** the pubic hair that a lover disturbs like the breeze shivering leaves on a tree.

VENUS'S GLOVE. The pudenda. In *Troilus and Cressida* Helen is said to 'swear by Venus's glove', which may have been a mild curse but is more likely to mean Helen is devoted to sex.

VIRGINAL. Not the physical state of purity (and how many of us can recollect that?) but a keyboard instrument – a small, legless spinet – that is played on in the way a seducer plays on a woman. In *The Winter's Tale* there is an image of a woman stroking a man's hand – she is 'virginalling on his palm', according to her jealous husband.

WAG YOUR TAIL, WAGTAIL. A **wagtail** is a slapper who wags her tail (vagina and rump) and any man who comes her way. The implication of **wag your tail** is that it's done for sheer fun and not with a commercial purpose.

WEAKNESS AND DEBILITY, THE MEANS OF. In *As You Like It* this phrase means masturbation and its popularly imagined after-effects.

WHAT. The vagina, according to *Love's Labour's Lost* and *Troilus and Cressida*.

WINCHESTER GOOSE. A whore, one operating out of the brothels between the Globe Theatre and London Bridge. All the properties there belonged to the Bishop of Winchester, so the working girls became known as **Winchester geese**.

WIND INSTRUMENT. The anus, especially when sounding off.

WITHERED PEAR. Virginity clung on to for far too long, according to *All's Well That Ends Well*: 'Your virginity, your old virginity, is like one of our French withered pears – it looks ill, it eats dryly; marry, 'tis a withered pear.'

WOODSMAN. A wencher and lecher, according to *Measure for Measure*.

WORLD. The word means a breast but, as the world is made of two hemispheres, **world** does duty for the breasts. In the poem *The Rape of Lucrece* the heroine's breasts are described like this:

> Her breasts, like ivory globes circled with blue,
> A pair of maiden worlds unconquered,
> Save of their lord no bearing yoke they knew ...

WRACK. Used in *Hamlet* to stand for defloration; Ophelia's father, Polonius, warns her that Prince Hamlet planned to **wrack** her.

YARD. The male member and a word socially acceptable from 1570 until about 1750. It never acquired the low-life quality that **prick, cock** and **tool** did.

8. DECENT OBSCURITY

In 1776 Edward Gibbon published the first volume of his *The History of the Decline and Fall of the Roman Empire*; the last volume appeared twelve years later but not until 1796 did Gibbon belatedly assure his readers that 'My English text is chaste, and all licentious passages are left in the obscurity of a learned language.' (This was parodied as 'the decent obscurity' by a magazine.)

This was a bit late for those readers who'd bought the book and been offended. It was also too late for anyone who'd snapped up the work to learn about the Romans' sordid habits. Unless the reader knew Latin, the naughty bits were unreadable. In those days the well-educated toffs were the only ones who got to read the randy stuff.

Here, for those without Latin, is a sample of what you're missing, along with some information on the Roman way of sex. All the stuff that *Gladiator* failed to show you.

The Romans were originally farmers and their economy depended on agriculture, thus interest in and affection for the countryside were part of their character. Rather like modern Britons, the Romans dreamed of a place in the country for long weekends and holidays.

Being farmers, the Romans worshipped fertility gods and goddesses. The chief god was Priapus, generally depicted as a grinning, bearded figure with considerably better than average sexual kit. He was the son of Bacchus and Venus, a lively combination of alcohol and lust. Priapus was also the name given to stout posts set up as boundary markers. As well as encouraging fertility, Priapus was supposed to scare off thieves and trespassers, presumably by making the villains feel so inferior that they slunk away blushing. Very large statues incorporated oil lamps in the phallus.

The well-endowed god was given a considerable number of affectionate names by his worshippers, including:

DEUS POSITO PUDORE. The god without shame. Well, if it's that size there's nothing to be ashamed about.

FICUS. Fig tree, because the wood is hard and the fruit looks very female when ripe. Dildos were made of fig or olive wood.

MEMBROSIOR AEQUO. Bigger-tooled than average. Words a Roman gent no doubt longed to hear his lady gasp.

RIGIDUS DEUS. Rigid god, for an obvious reason.

SALAX DEUS. The lecherous god. Look, you have your hobbies, let him have his.

The Romans thought up particular names to honour Priapus's outstanding feature, such as:

ARMA VENTRIS. Belly weapons, referring to the full set of cock and balls.

CAPUT LUBRICUM. Lubricious head.

CONTUS PEDALIS. The twelve-inch pole – often a modest specimen on statues.

HASTA RUDIS. The rude or rough spear.

INGUEN OBSCAENUM. Obscene groin.

MENTULA MAGNA. Great organ, always ready to be played.

NERVUS TENTUS. The stiff nerve, an image still with us.

PALUS RUBER. The bloodstained pole – or perhaps the blood-swollen pole.

PARS MAJOR. The greater part. Greater than most other parts in those parts, that is.

PYRAMIS. The pyramid, a shape popular after Antony connected with Cleopatra.

VIRILE PARS. The virile part.

These endearments and compliments were generally reserved for the outstanding god; there were plenty of words to apply to the mortal male's favourite among his organs:

ANGUIS. A snake, which could be a sign of good fortune. It has been claimed that some thrill-chasing Roman women used live snakes as dildos.

ARBOR. A tree. The speaker probably pictured some tall and tough growth rather than a small bush.

CAUDA TURGENS. A swollen tail, just the thing to wag at the girls in the Forum.

COLCATA CUSPIS. A pointed stem.

CLAVUS CUPIDINIS. Cupid's rudder, an ancestor of **Cupid's battering ram** (see Chapter 3).

CUCUMIS. A cucumber, one of the most popular dishes in ancient Roman; the image has pleased men so much that it's continued in use to the present day.

Anguis

FABA. A bean or one of the testicles, depending on the context.

FALX. A sickle, which was not only an agricultural implement, but in the hands of the enemies of Rome, such as the Thracians, a fearsome weapon.

GLADIUS. A sword – from which gladiators took their name – and another image that has survived over the centuries. The Romans used many types of sword, including the *ensis*, *machaera* and *mucro*. The cavalry used a long, heavy weapon called the *spatha*. The Roman penis had a range of weapons to pick a name from.

LIGO. A mattock – that is, a sort of pickaxe with a broad cutting head.

LORUM IN AQUA. Wet leather, which may not be a compliment.

MALA. Apples, also the testicles.

MONSTRUM. A monster, which could be boasting, or a factual description of an unpleasant organ.

NATRIX. Either a whip or a variety of water snake – take your pick.

PALUS. A large wooden stake, though perhaps not as large as the owner thinks.

PESSULUS. A heavy bolt or the penis.

POMA. Another word for apples, so another word for testicles, too.

PONDUS. A heavy weight, though whether that applied to the whole man or just one feature is unclear.

PUGIO. A dagger, carried by a Roman legionary for infighting. Or perhaps something else he carried ready for action.

RADIUS. A rod, size not specified but presumed to be long and thick.

RASTER. A hoe – the Romans liked their rural and horticultural images.

RUTABULUM. But they didn't mind household comparisons; **rutabulum** means an oven rake.

SERPENS. A serpent, the ancestor of the dread one-eyed trouser snake.

SICA. A knife or dagger.

TAURUS. A bull and an image that has outlasted the Roman Empire by many centuries.

THYRSUS. A staff. It was originally a vine- or ivy-draped wand carried by Bacchus and his worshippers.

TRIEMBOLUM. A large penis, though who did the measuring and set the standards is unknown.

TRUNCUS. A tree. As with **arbor**, we can assume that something on the lines of an oak rather than a dwarf rhododendron was in the owner's mind.

VILIA MEMBRA. The vile parts, a phrase popular with eunuchs and Puritans.

VIRGULA. A stick or rod.

VOMER. A ploughshare and highly appropriate in a society that called the female sex organs **ager**, meaning a field.

Of course, not every Roman was well equipped and the Latin language deals with the lack some men (and their women) felt:

ALUTA. This means soft leather, the kind of flaccid tassel no man longs to own.

BETA. A beet (as in root vegetable), but an elderly and wizened specimen.

BIPENNA. A very small penis, the 'ickle prickle' of coarse jokes.

CHRYSION. A miniature organ of little use to anyone, not even the owner.

Vomer

CURCULIO. A weevil or corn worm; the sort of agricultural pest that joins the Young Farmers these days.

PANNUCEA MENTULA. A shrivelled penis, the victim of overuse or old age.

PASSER. A tricky word this, meaning a sparrow. That could be an insult, given a sparrow's size; on the other hand, the bird has a reputation for randy energy and all-weather copulation, so perhaps it's a compliment.

PIPPINA. This is an insult, however, being derived from a word imitating the chirrup of a little bird and describing a tiny tool.

SALAPUTIUM. Another way of referring to a male organ that is less than satisfactory in size and performance.

SICULA VEL PARVA SICA. A small dagger and an unkind comparison.

STRUTHEUM. Another name for a sparrow. See **passer**.

VASCULUM. A little vessel, perhaps eyebath-sized or maybe smaller.

VERETILLUM. A minute sexual part, barely worth acknowledging.

The Romans had a wide range of names for the female sexual parts, such as *alvus* and *delphys*, for the womb. Two other words for the womb are in use today: uterus and viscera (though this now means intestines). Vagina, which meant a sheath, and vulva, a wrapper or container, are still with us today. They spoke and wrote about the *amphidaeum* and *cadurca* (the labia) and *murton* or *murtum*, meaning the clitoris. They also called the clitoris *Venus prodigiosa* and *veretrum muliebre*. *Femen* indicated the upper area of the thigh and *femur summum* the very top of the thigh where the genitalia (also Latin) are located.

Their equivalent of cunt was *cunnus*; the *cunnus consule natus* was that of a noblewoman, while a bony cunt, *cunnus osseus*, indicated an old lady. Prostitutes were marked by a *cunnus albus* (white cunt) and there was even a talkative variety, *cunnus garrulous,* which made a lot of squelching sounds during intercourse.

As you would expect of a farming nation, a lot of the terms are drawn from the farm and garden, landscape features like caves and comparisons with fruit:

AGER. A field and one with acreage that includes the vagina and buttocks.

ANTRUM MULIEBRE. The female cave or cavern.

ARVUM. Another word for a field but restricted to the vagina.

BARATHRUM. A cave.

CAMPUS. An open space, a plain or even a parade ground. Where do you find a university? In the middle of its campus, of course. An expanded version of the term was *campus venereus* meaning 'the plain of pleasure'.

CAVERNA. A cavern or cave.

CAVUM. Take a guess … you're right, it's a cave. No one ever accused the Romans of excessive imagination.

CRYPTA. A crypt, a sinister word that may indicate a certain male nervousness.

FICUS. This could be used of a vagina, but more often it meant piles as in haemorrhoids.

FOLLICULUS. A pea pod or the husk of a fruit, and not the most flattering of comparisons for the female sexual parts.

FOSSA. A ditch and a metaphor covering both the vulva and the buttock cleft of a male whore. *Fossula* was a little ditch, and a *fosser* (ditch-digger) was a lecher.

FUNDUS. A farm. The word seems to have implied the whole pubic region and the bottom.

HIATUS. A cleft or slit. The word has shifted into English to indicate a pause or gap; I don't think it has a sexual meaning these days, however.

HORTUS, HORTUS MULIEBRIS. A garden/woman's garden and an image that has been used over the centuries by different cultures. The Romans named several different kinds of garden; there was *hortus Cupidinis* (Cupid's garden) and the *hortus conclusus* (the enclosed or walled garden). The *hortus Hesperidum* was the

Hortus

Garden of the Hesperides, where apples grew that could make you immortal if you ate them.

ILLA. Just means 'that', the nameless, the part we dare not speak of. They were prudes at times, the old Romans.

MARISCA. Latin for a fig, a metaphor for the anus that has appeared many times over the centuries. The best figs came from the island of Chios and Roman poets were fond of comparing a boy's anus to a Chian fig. **Marisca**, an inferior variety of fig, was reserved for the female anus.

MATULA. This is hardly flattering; the word indicates a large bowl of a sort kept under the bed. Yes, the po, gazzunda, Cromwell's skull or whatever you call a chamber-pot.

OSTIUM. An entrance or gateway.

PENETRALIA. The inmost part of the body (and the most sacred area of a temple) reached via the **ostium** or perhaps the *fores* – another word for a gateway.

PLANTARIA. The word means ferns but stands for the pubic hairs.

PROPUDIUM FISSILE. Uncomplimentary and prudish, the phrase means shameful cleft.

PUTEUS. A well, and an obvious image for the vagina but a paradox for later ages singing the song 'Ding-dong bell, pussy's down the well'.

RECESSUS. A nook or cranny, still in use as the English 'recess'.

RIMA. A chink or narrow slot.

SALTUS. A very narrow pathway.

SCROBS. Another word for a ditch; not a compliment.

SULCUS. The furrow a ploughshare cuts in the earth, a very agricultural word.

VALLIS FEMORUM. The valley between the thighs, an example of precise location work by the Roman surveyors. They used other place terms like *media* (in the middle), and *locus* (a place).

VENEREUM ARVUM. The field of pleasure.

VINEA. A vineyard, a source of wealth and great pleasure.

Other terms for the female genitals often sound like modern slang, though seasoned with Roman culture:

ANULARE, ANNULUS. A ring and an image that has endured. (See **Carvel's ring** and **ring** in Chapter 2.)

AQUAE FONS. A fountain of water, often the central and most treasured feature of ancient gardens and the ladies in them. Another name that reappeared after many centuries.

ARA VOLUPTATIS. The altar of pleasure, located in the **penetralia** of a temple.

BUCCA. A facial cheek, soft and swelling.

BULGA. A leather bag or bottle – is this flattering or not? Leather was a superior material to clay in times when glass might be rare and costly.

CADURCUM. A cosy domestic comparison for the vagina, **cadurcum** meant a coverlet for a bed.

CELOX. A boat – from the shape or the hollowness?

CONCHA. This is a shell, one of the kind with ribbed pink lips beside the vertical opening. The shell-shaped pasta *conchiglie* may celebrate the female body.

CRISTA. A crest, perhaps a reminder of the hair crests on a soldier's helmet.

CUSTON. A perfume bottle. Roman women were fond of scents and would spend large amounts of money on rare perfumes, often imported from India.

DELTA. The Greek letter D, which looks like this: Δ. The comparison here is obvious.

FONS. A simple fountain.

HUMIDUS LACUS. A warm or humid lake, ideal for skinny-dipping.

HYSTERA. The womb, which could be overstimulated, according to Roman and Greek doctors, and make women hysterical.

LUBRICUM FEMUR. The lubricious or lascivious thigh, a feature much admired by the Roman male, though never described in precise detail.

Custon

MEATUM VENERIS. The passage of pleasure, Venus's foyer, the vagina and adjacent features.

MELINA. Latin for honey. This could mean either the taste of a woman or the sweetness of touch. It was an endearment engraved on rings and other jewellery by the Romans and Greeks.

NAVIS. A ship, larger than a **celox**.

OPPIDULUM. This means a small town and may not be flattering; towns have many inhabitants coming and going about commercial business. On the other hand, a town is a centre of civilisation and fun.

PARMA. A valve; a simple image.

PORCUS. A pig, which may seem rude, but the pig was an important sacrificial animal and an essential part of some religious rites.

PORTUS. A port, a safe place, a haven where the weary traveller could find comfort and warmth.

PTERYGOMATA. The labia.

RENES. The loins, meaning the whole lap and all the pudenda.

SINUS. The breast.

TUBUS. A pipe or tube, and a basic image for the vagina.

The use of agricultural and gardening images was carried into the Roman sexual vocabulary, as you would expect:

ARARE. To plough a field and a woman.

DEGLUBERE. Fellatio and/or masturbation; the literal Latin meaning is to shell something, e.g. shelling peas.

FODERE. To have sex with a woman and to dig the earth or plough a furrow.

MOLERE. To grind, a verb that is still in use as a sexual term in this century. A *mollitor* was the man doing the grinding.

RIGARE. To irrigate and water a garden or fields, and to discharge semen.

ROS. The dew, and a poetic name for semen.

SARRIRE. Intercourse with a woman; down on the farm it meant hoeing and weeding.

After a hard day weeding or talking in the Forum the Romans relaxed in their famous baths. Naked bathing was commonplace but the sexes were separated and watched by morals police. After the bath and massage the men might endure a shave, done with an iron razor and no shaving soap to soften the beard, just warm water. Minor nicks and gashes were treated with a splash of vinegar. Other body hair might be removed – Julius Caesar used hot walnut shells to remove leg hair – but only rent-boys had all their body hair removed.

Roman ladies went in for cosmetics in a big way. They slapped on white lead mixtures and powdered chalk to make their arms and necks look paler, and coloured their cheeks with red ochre. Red wine lees served as lipstick and various blends of carbons and kohl were used as eye make-up. Hair extensions and wigs were in regular use.

When it came to making love the Romans liked to have settings that encouraged them; bedrooms featured erotic paintings and statues, as well as plates and cups with sexual scenes on them. The emperor Tiberius was famous for his collection of erotic pictures and books; he employed teams of sex performers called *spintriae* or *spinthriae* (meaning bracelets), who formed human chains, each member connected to the next in one way or another. At times groups of three sported in front of Tiberius to encourage him to get an erection.

Spintriae

One of the most popular sexual positions, which appears over and over in Roman erotica, is the woman astride the man, called *mulier equitans* (the woman riding), or *inequitatio* (being ridden on, and known as a **St George** in later days; see Chapter 5). Roman males considered this method distinctly naughty; poets churned out verses on the topic. According to the philosopher Lucretius, a woman in this position could avoid pregnancy by lifting herself clear of the man before he came.

The mounted posture was a favourite with Roman prostitutes (and their clients, of course) and they had a strong professional need to avoid conception. The whores became famously expert at riding men and varying their speed, using wagglings (*fluctuo* in Latin) and buckings (*crisso*) to exhaust customers.

What they enjoyed in the whorehouse the men wanted at home, too, and Roman ladies soon learnt the new posture. (It is interesting to note that Roman married women were supposed to be virtuous and spend their time spinning and raising children. They weren't trusted to go out and buy the family meals; the men took care of all the food shopping.)

As well as the *inequitatio* the Romans adopted the missionary position and enjoyed sex doggy fashion, though they compared it to the mating of tortoises rather than dogs. It was believed sex on all fours was the best way to conceive; Lucretius stated that women absorbed sperm more effectively in that position.

Emperor Augustus enjoyed his murderous wife Livia in that manner, even when she was pregnant.

Tollere pedes was the term for a woman lying on her back and raising her legs to open herself to her lover; the poets (male) believed this was a method women found particularly pleasing. In *supponere femur* the woman lay on her side and placed her thigh over the man; this was supposed to be the most comfortable posture for a woman. It was also one that allowed her to enjoy anal and vaginal intercourse at the same time, if she was into threesomes. *Mulier sedens* could be the woman lying on the bed while the man stands and raises her legs to his shoulders, or a standing couple with the woman wrapping her legs round the man and being supported by him.

Anal intercourse (*paedico*) with his wife and mistress was considered simply one more sexual option for the Roman male. In fact, he might grow angry if his wife failed to cooperate; the poet Martial penned some peevish lines to his wife, pointing out that the wives of famous men had obliged them so why wouldn't she let him do what he wanted? Elsewhere Martial praised a woman who allowed him access to her buttocks. A popular move was called *siphniassare*, which was inserting a finger in the anus during intercourse.

Anal sex with other men was regarded with some disdain, though mythology and Roman history offered plenty of examples, for instance Julius Caesar with King Nicomedes of Bithynia. It seems that being the passive partner or making use of male slaves led to mocking comments and even prosecution, but enjoying freeborn men was acceptable.

The Romans had mixed views on oral sex. There are pictures of couples enjoying cunnilingus, fellatio and 69; Tiberius had a large painting of Atalanta giving the hero Meleager a **blow job** hanging in his imperial bedroom. The emperor was noted for his oral practices with women (there were rude songs on the subject) and for being fellated by boys called 'minnows' while swimming in his pool.

But the poets and many politicians described fellatio as vile and obscene; fellatio was called *stuprum oris* (defilement of the mouth), *offendere buccam* (offending the cheek) and *capitalis luxus* (debauching the head). One reason for the distaste was that the usual Roman greeting was a kiss on the lips.

Cunnilingus was popular with the Romans and Greeks, though it is seldom shown in Roman erotic pictures. Though popular, it was denounced by writers of the time, who wrote of 'cunt-lickers with foul breath' and young men with pale faces, worn out by the vice, and older men with their beards stained by vaginal secretions. It was claimed that men only resorted to oral sex when their penises could no longer function or, in the case of the priests of some cults, when they'd been castrated.

Much of the hostility sounds like the anti-masturbation propaganda of later centuries; though the Romans were less grumpy about self-stimulation, they did not wholly approve of it. The term masturbation may be derived from the Latin **manu stuprare** (to defile using the hand), which is hardly a positive start. According to mythology, Mercury showed his son Pan how to masturbate after Pan lost his mistress Echo. Pan then taught some shepherds the pleasure and the good news spread through the world. There are frequent mentions of it in Latin literature; the poet Juvenal was not in favour of schoolboys giving one another a helping hand, and Martial mentions slaves masturbating as they watch their master and mistress screwing.

The most public display was recorded by Plutarch; he described the philosopher Diogenes standing in the marketplace masturbating. When the end came Diogenes said, 'I wish to god I could satisfy my hunger by rubbing my stomach.'

Don't get the idea the whole of Roman society was busy indulging in red-hot sexual orgies night after night. There were some strict laws in place and at times they were harshly enforced. Much of our notion of Roman sexual games is based on the activities of the rich and privileged – especially the most privileged man in their world: the emperor. Incest was punished by a painful death – but not if you were Caligula, who enjoyed each of his three sisters in turn, or Nero, who bedded his mother. Nero also married a boy he had tried to turn into a girl by castration. Galba, who replaced Nero, celebrated the news of Nero's death by taking his favourite man to bed. Some courtiers, senior army officers and ambitious politicians disapproved of the ways the emperors behaved and murdered them – though not just because of their sex lives.

One legacy of Rome and the Latin language is our medical terminology for body parts; vulva, uterus and vagina are obvious examples; there is also the shared imagery of sexual acts, for like the Romans later societies have talked of ploughing furrows, compared women to caves, fields and gardens, and the penis to a cucumber, beet and dagger.

There you have it, folks, the Roman games that *Gladiator* failed to feature. It's surprising how many of the Latin images have lived on in other languages until recent decades. The English language is crammed with fine old words and phrases – start using them now and add mystery and spice to your chat-up lines and pillow talk. Not to mention the names you can shout at any maggot-galloper who gets in your way.